Waking Dreams

Waking Dreams

Imagination in Psychotherapy and Everyday Life

Allan Frater

TransPersonal
Press

TransPersonal Press
(*a Kaminn Media imprint*)
272 Bath Street
Glasgow G2 4JR
Scotland
transpersonalpress.com

A CIP record for this title is available from the British Library.

ISBN 978-1-912698-08-0 (print)
ISBN 978-1-912698-09-7 (ebook)

Cover Illustration © Keith Robinson 2021

Edited by Nicky Leach
Text design and layout by Thierry Bogliolo
This book was typeset in Calluna.

Printed, bound and distributed by Ingram Spark

Contents

This book is dedicated to my family.

The modern vision of ourselves and the world has stultified
our imaginations . . . .What is needed is a revisioning,
a fundamental shift of perspective out of
that soulless predicament we call modern consciousness.

—James Hillman

Introduction

We need a therapy of imagination, one that respects it not as a means toward cognitive understanding but as valuable in its own right.

—Steven K. Levine[1]

Our approach to the imaging is predetermined by our idea of it.

—James Hillman[2]

To read a book on imagination can be a risky endeavour. If the aim is to have a more imaginative life, as it is in this book, caution needs to be taken.

There is no shortage, in these rational-minded times, of books that purport to explain what images mean—texts that translate memories, dreams and fantasies into symbolic representations of inner psychodynamics, the narrative templates of Greek myths, and the internalization of childhood history; maps of imagination, developmental pathways, escape routes from nightmares and anxieties. All of which is fine, so far as it goes.

There is a time and a place for analytical thinking. It allows us to step back and gain perspective, but it is not to be mistaken for living an imaginative life. The map is not the territory, as the saying goes.

In the same way that reading about expeditions across the polar ice caps is an armchair exploration from the safety and comfort of home, so too are clever explanations and theories about images not to be confused with the up-close, imaginative participation of story and dream. However, much of the psychological literature is decidedly unclear on this distinction between thinking and imagining; a muddled approach that assumes imagination to be an elaborate puzzle, images as ideas.

Interpretation alone rarely leads to lasting transformation. The neurotic Woody Allen– type character, with lots of insight from years of therapy but no actual change in their behaviour, is a therapeutic cliché, a cartoon exaggeration of the impasse that occurs when analytical thinking eclipses the kind of imagination needed to turn insight into action.

An imagination that bridges desire into living realization in the world is little understood. Mainstream psychological theory and practice are predicated upon an "inner" idea of imagination quite separate from the world—an understanding of "images in the mind . . . not present to the senses"; perhaps at times a creative "faculty", but often a pejorative "imaginary" or "fantasy"; a psychological interiority not to be confused with objective reality. As we shall see, though, this is at best a partial understanding. An inward focus and abstracted distance from the activity of images in everyday life that make it harder to imagine new ways of being and relationships.

This book offers a noninterpretative approach that focuses upon the quality of attention and skills needed to be imaginative rather than trying to figure out what images mean. It is something of a practical guidebook intended for those more intrepid readers who want to enter into and participate in the activity of images.

This is the book I would have liked to receive on starting my training as a psychotherapist. At that time, the imaginative richness of my life—that elusive sense of story and play and possibility—was fading. The surface images of everyday life—a walk in the park, a conversation with a neighbour, a cat sitting high up in a tree— were becoming ever emptier and weightless; like the scrolled-past content on my phone, no longer able to impinge upon and meaningfully touch me. I felt ever less absorbed and able to focus, seldom really feeling *there* anymore.

What was going on?

Perhaps it was just part of getting older, the latest in a series of losses all the way back to childhood chat with imaginary friends? Perhaps it was the alienating effects of online technologies. Perhaps depression? Whatever the reason, I wanted back those moments when an image would capture my whole attention—a russet autumnal sunset or even just a tattered plastic bag flapping in a hawthorn hedge, moments when I would stand and gaze, seduced into an implicit meaningfulness in just being alive.

I wanted that sensual imagining back again, and signing up for a psychotherapy training programme had been an attempt to get some practical guidance and advice. In a way it worked—just not quite as I expected.

It soon became apparent that learning to be a psychotherapist was not a direct route to the recovery of imagination. How to imagine was rather taken for granted. The emphasis was upon how best to use images. Imagination was assumed to be a kind of machine, something that could be controlled to manipulate psychological change. A lot of time was spent applying image-based techniques using carefully chosen symbols and stories that produced image puzzles that were explained using a lexicon of "sub-personality", "super-ego", and "shadow".

While some of these ideas were practically useful and intellectually stimulating they were not helping me rediscover the imaginative life I had lost, at least not directly. In the dim corners of my mind questions slowly began to take shape—questions that arose despite rather than because of what I was taught, questions that grew in strength and clarity as I pursued them into clinical work and then a teaching career.

Over the years, many clients, students, and colleagues have helped test out, articulate, and refine answers that eventually led to the image-centric approach I now present here in book form. Due to the origins of the book, many of the ideas and examples come from a psychotherapeutic context. While this will most obviously be of interest to therapists, what follows has been written with a general-interest reader firmly in mind. No expert understanding is required. Technical academic language has largely been avoided, not least because it undermines imagining, and where used is explained in a straightforward fashion. In addition, much of the material is grounded in examples and exercises that go beyond a conventional therapeutic context. As the subtitle suggests, this is a book about imagination in psychotherapy *and* everyday life. It is for anyone who wants to enhance their imaginative life.

The main requirement for the enhancement of imagination is spending time with images, from watching clouds and sunsets to visiting art galleries and reading novels; in other words, approaching images on their own level, unmediated by any theoretical framework. To this end, the book has an experiential emphasis. In particular, the practice of "waking dreams" is presented across a series of chapters, each of which explores a different aspect of the principles and skills needed to enhance imaginative life.

A waking dream is the exploration of the borderland consciousness that lies in between waking and dreaming, such as happens on gradually waking from sleep when the dream world continues to feel present alongside an awareness of lying in bed. Usually, these spontaneous waking dreams are of short duration but with practice we can learn to recreate the necessary conditions for a sustained exploration.

The subtle imaginal attention of this waking/dreaming state, also known as "active imagination" and "guided imagery", will be familiar to actors, writers, artists and other explorers of creative imagination, as well as those psychotherapists, counsellors, coaches, and clinical psychologists who draw upon image-based orientations, such as psychosynthesis, gestalt, art therapy, and psychodrama. While it may seem familiar, waking-dream practice in this book goes beyond a standard presentation by developing two hitherto underexplored opportunities within this practice.

The first novel opportunity is an exploration of imagining in the moment. The obvious advantage of a waking dream over a sleeping dream (in which the surroundings convince entirely and only upon waking do we recognize it as a dream) is that consciousness continues while imagining within the dreamscape. The blend of waking and dreaming is a real-time interaction with images that grants the opportunity to become familiar with not just the content of *what* we imagine but also the process of *how* we imagine.

This is a somewhat novel emphasis because waking dreams or similar imaginative methods are often presented as no different from sleeping dreams: a means to generate image content that is then studied for psychological insight. This retrospective stance focuses on what images mean rather than on an experiential, up-close interaction with images on their own level; in other words, thinking about images as opposed to imagining alongside and with images, the effect of which is a cognitive distance from the immediacy of imaginative experience.

I will show that an emphasis on in-the-moment waking dreams serves as the basis for the transformative and healing effects of imagination. An everyday example is the lift in mood we feel after watching a movie. We leave the cinema having being moved by the language of images rather than ideas that explain why we feel better. Indeed, such an interpretative approach might be a hindrance, eclipsing the effects of imaginative experience, as is well understood by the importance of experiential work in contemporary psychotherapy.

This contemporary experiential work focuses mostly upon embodied feeling states rather than images and imagination; however, the difficulty, even for experienced therapists, is that the alienating effects of modern lifestyles foster a general absence of bodily and feeling awareness, which often makes direct enquiries in this regard unproductive. The advantage of the image-based experiential work presented here is that the ability to describe and interact with images is a level of awareness readily available to most people and, as we shall discover, also an indirect route into embodied emotional experience.

The second novel opportunity developed in the book is an exploration of everyday life as an ongoing "eyes-wide-open" waking dream. The point of waking dreams is not just to get good at an introspective "eyes-closed" study of "images in the mind"; the wider aim is to carry this imaginal perception over into "normal" life as an ongoing "eyes-wide-open" waking dream.

In the book, I will show how the images and themes encountered in "eyes-closed" waking dreams are relatable to relationships with real-world people, places, and things. Of course, this is not to suggest that a scary-dragon image in an "eyes-closed" waking dream will literally be found afterwards crouched behind the garden fence, but rather, that the waking-dream story of the dragon will be an imaginal background or parallel pattern to real-world situations.

I will show how this patterning allows for connections to be made between seemingly disparate contexts—for example, the dragon image, a boss, an annoying neighbour, a movie character, and a historical caregiver—and that learning to notice these patterns is what cultivates an imaginal sensitivity to the activity of images in everyday life, a sensitivity that can then employ the same principles and practices developed in "eyes-closed" waking dreams to the reimagining of self and world.

As I will show, this second development of waking dream practice provides a basis for an image-centric approach to generic psychotherapy work as an "eyes-wide-open" waking dream. While the images found in memories, in-the-moment perceptions, and future fantasies constitute the raw material of any psychotherapy, conventional approaches often treat images as of only secondary importance. Typically, after a brief description of any such imagery, the therapist will focus upon the feeling and thought responses rather than work directly with the images themselves, asking questions such as "How does it make you feel?" or "How do you understand it?", thus, allowing imagining to be eclipsed by thinking and feeling.

The image-centric approach I sketch out in these pages will show how feelings, thoughts, and body sensations can all be included within therapeutic work that maintains its primary focus upon images and imagining. Most directly applicable to this image-centric treatment will be art-based therapies, such as drawing, modelling, puppets, sand trays, drama, and movement, and popular image-based techniques, such as Gestalt "empty chair", subpersonalities, and family constellation work.

Beyond this more direct application, I will also explore bread-and-butter therapeutic work using client memories, future fantasies, phenomenological in-the-moment processing, and the "dreaming-up" of the transference relationship in the context of "eyes-wide-open" waking dreams—not as the invention of a new modality but as a way of using waking-dream principles to clarify the role of imagination already present within such experiential therapeutic work.

The more experiential Waking Dream chapters are alternated with a series of theoretical chapters. First-hand interaction with images is important, but in itself is not enough. What is also needed is the clearing of a conceptual space that validates imaginative experience. This is important because much of contemporary psychotherapeutic theory and practice does not ask, let alone answer, basic questions such as: What exactly is imagination? What is going on when we imagine? How can we imagine more fully? And why would we want to?

Instead of shying away from these key questions, this book turns directly towards them. As the psychotherapist Mary Watkins writes: "It is ironic that those psychologies which seem to give the greatest respect to the imaginal have not inquired into the subject of what they have imagined of imagining."[3]

What we imagine of imagination matters. The above questions are not just a theoretical but also a practical matter. To answer them is to ever more fully notice, validate, and enhance imagining. To ignore them is to perpetuate assumptions that limit imagining.

For instance, to assume that imagination is a psychological interiority, or "inner imagination", blinkers us to its activity in everyday life; to assume that imagination is about visual images precludes noticing its presence in embodied sensory experience; and to assume pejoratively that imagination is "imaginary" or "made-up" pushes us away from considering its creative benefits. In order to work through these and many other assumptions, the theoretical chapters present a critical discussion of the conceptual frameworks and metaphors of imagination.

The theoretical discussion takes two converging critical perspectives. The first is a phenomenological enquiry that tests the conventional theoretical assumption of "inner imagination" against the experiential ground it purports to address.

I will use the viewing of a Van Gogh painting as an example of the lived experience, or "phenomenon", of imagining. In reflecting upon this example, I will show that imagination, rather than "images in the mind", is experientially an embodied act of everyday perception (chapter 1) in which we find ourselves immersed within an encompassing image environment (chapter 3) as if it is alive, or animate (chapter 5).

The second critical perspective considers the place of metaphor, the ability to imagine one thing "as if" it is another, in the understanding and experience of imagination. I will trace back the limiting effects of technology in shaping how we imagine (chapter 7) to the historical origins of the "mind-as-machine" metaphor still embedded in many commonly used psychological theories, and then consider the possibilities of a theory of imagination rooted in ecological rather than mechanical metaphors by drawing upon the integration of psychotherapy with contemporary perspectives from complexity theory (chapter 9) and fractal geometry (chapter 11). Finally, in the concluding chapter (chapter 13), I will draw together the various strands of the critical discussion to propose a transpersonal, or "beyond-the-personal" imagination as a framework that releases imagination from the dualistic assumptions of 20th century psychology. The result is a theory of imagination more closely aligned with and supportive of the actual phenomenological richness and complexity of imaginative experience.

The critical discussion draws upon and develops ideas from many sources. An inevitable influence has been my initial therapy training in the psychosynthesis of Roberto Assagioli.[4] In no way a general introduction to psychosynthesis, the book can be read as a sympathetic development of the hidden potential within the many image-based applications of classical psychosynthesis, many of which have been taken up by other therapies but have received very little critical attention or modification over the years. In particular, the transpersonal context of psychosynthesis— "trans" in this context meaning "beyond"—is made explicit to offer an application of image-based work that goes beyond the theoretical constraints of a purely personal or intrapsychic psychology.

Another key influence for me has been the great Swiss psychoanalyst and early transpersonal theorist Carl Jung, who wrote that "Psyche is image" and "Every psychic process is an image and imagining".[5]

The book particularly draws upon the work of those post-Jungians who have developed his image-centric approach to psychotherapy, such as James Hillman, Mary Watkins, Robert Bosnak, and Russel Lockhart. The frequent usage of the term "imaginal" derives from this post-Jungian influence. The term "imaginal" was coined by Sufi scholar Henry Corbin from the Latin root *imago* and has been widely adopted as a means to convey a reality of imaginative experience that avoids the connotations of "imaginary" as unreal, made-up, or nonexistent.

Further influences that have helped me sketch out an approach to imagination beyond the therapeutic consulting room have come from ecopsychology and anthropology. While ecopsychology rarely mentions imagination, the writings of Theodor Roszak, Jerome Bernstein, Andy Fisher and Nick Totton have nevertheless helped shape the image-centric reconnection to the more-than-human world presented here. In a similar earth-centric vein, the cultural ecologist David Abram and anthropologists Hugh Brody, David Graeber, and Sean Kane have contributed to an understanding of an "everyday" imagination outside the bounds of both conventional psychotherapy and contemporary culture.

One of my favourite lines from Roberto Assagioli is "When will and imagination come into conflict, imagination wins".[6] His point is that imagination is an important precursor to change; good ideas and motivations are not enough. Without the ability to imagine those ideas as realistic opportunities, we go with the flow of the familiar rather than step into the uncertainty of the new. In order to change, an imaginative bridge is needed in order to turn hopes and dreams from frustrated inner fantasies into real-world actions and events.

In this view, therapy is primarily an act of imagination. To the extent imaginative possibilities can be engaged with a new "will", a way forward can emerge, one that is able to carry ideas and dreams into expression in the world. This book provides the theoretical and practical basis for such an image-centric approach. The following chapters are full of ideas, examples, and exercises that address the place of imagining in the consulting room and beyond—an imagination for psychotherapy and everyday life.

1. Stephen K. Levine, *Trauma, Tragedy, Therapy: The Arts and Human Suffering* (London: Jessica Kingsley, 2009), 19.

2. James Hillman, *Re-Visioning Psychology* (New York: Harper Perennial, 1992), 39.

3. Mary Watkins, *Waking Dreams* (Thompson, CT: Spring Publications, 2003), 143.

4. http://psychosynthesistrust.org.uk

5. Benjamin Sells, ed. *Working with Images: The Theoretical Base of Archetypal Psychology* (Thompson, CT: Spring Publications, 2000), 5.

6. Roberto Assagioli, *Psychosynthesis: A Manual of Principles and Techniques* (London: Thorsons, 1993), 144.

Chapter 1

Embodied Imagination

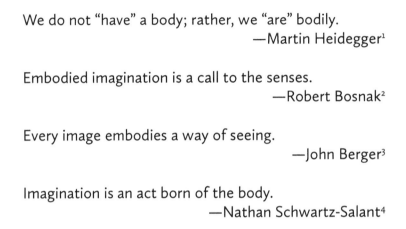

We do not "have" a body; rather, we "are" bodily.
—Martin Heidegger[1]

Embodied imagination is a call to the senses.
—Robert Bosnak[2]

Every image embodies a way of seeing.
—John Berger[3]

Imagination is an act born of the body.
—Nathan Schwartz-Salant[4]

What is imagination? How do we imagine more fully? Why would we want to imagine? These are the core questions that weave together all the points made in this book.

To begin to find some answers we start with a simple description of what actually happens when we imagine. The experiential ground of imagining will be the basis upon which we build a practical understanding. This might appear an obvious strategy, and yet, common theories of imagination in both the academic and mainstream literature are not at all based on an experiential approach. This leads to a problematic set of quite abstract and alienating ideas that restrict imaginative life, a topsy-turvy situation that we now set about reversing in the search for a theory of imagination that accurately reflects the experiential ground it purports to address.

The simple description of imagining we shall be exploring is what happens when looking at a painting. For no special reason, I have chosen a painting by Vincent Van Gogh titled *The Bedroom*, as seen on my 11-inch laptop screen. Admittedly this makes for a personal account. No doubt others will find variations and differences from my experience. However, the aim is to reflect not so much on the content of what I imagined—it could have been any other painting, photograph, memory, or even a view out of a window—but rather to describe and reflect upon the process of what happens when we imagine, a process that will be shown to be common to all.

With a period of uninterrupted time, I sat at my desk to focus on the painting. It was a chance to slow down and discover what satisfying, enriching contact with art involves and how it can be enhanced. This is what happened:

> *I try to focus but it is not easy. Is this it? Boring!*
>
> *I want to know what the painting is about. If I were in an art gallery, I would be reading the blurb by now, but I resist doing an internet search and keep on looking.*
>
> *I see a small room with lilac walls and a wooden floor, a narrow bed along the wall, two upright chairs, and a washstand. A white towel hangs from a nail behind the door. The spacious simplicity is calming. I notice my thoughts slowing down.*
>
> *The bed has been neatly made up, the covers folded over, and the pillows puffed up against the headboard. I imagine the bed being made –a routine tidiness, a care being taken.*
>
> *The window glass is opaque, with deep green light. I can hear a swish of lush foliage growing nearby. A cooling breeze trickles in through the window, which is open just a crack.*
>
> *Above the bed are two portraits. One is a man, the other a woman. Both look directly at me and seem nonplussed at my presence, wondering what I am doing in their room.*
>
> *I feel like I've had enough. I should probably move on before anyone comes back and finds me in their bedroom.*

The imagined painting relied upon scanning my eyes across the laptop screen. Only on the basis of this bodily involvement did the painting come to life imaginatively. Imagination is an embodied experience—"embodied" from the French *incarné*, which means "of meat"—dependent upon sensory attention. And yet what I imagined was not a series of pixels or even a collection of brush strokes. I imagined a room with a bed, tables, and chairs and an atmosphere and mood distinct from the actual room in which I was sitting by my desk. Somehow the raw sensory screen data was turned into something more than its merely physical or objective reality. As the cultural ecologist David Abram writes:

> That which we call imagination is from the first an attribute of the senses themselves; imagination is not a separate mental faculty (as we so often assume) but is rather the way the senses themselves have of throwing themselves beyond what is immediately given.[5]

Imagination transformed the immediately given flat, static, and inert laptop screen into a three-dimensional, temporal-dynamic, and living place filled with details that were not directly depicted. The foliage outside the window, the breeze passing through it, and the felt gaze of the portraits were all imagined elements not immediately given by the painting. As James Hillman observes: "Images are not the same as optical pictures."[6] That which is imagined is not simply an empirical reproduction of what is physically sensed. In the same way that a movie-projector colours and animates a blank and stationary cinema screen, so too does imagination project or throw itself into the world and fill in the gaps in our sense impressions.

The imagined Van Gogh was a result of my imagination filling in the gaps between the pixels on the screen, such that it became a recognizable and meaningful narrative scenario, a projection of my subjective experience onto the painting. And yet the movie-projector metaphor does not quite fit. Imaginative projection is not entirely subjective. Once again, David Abram makes this clear:

> The notion of "projection" fails to account for what it is about certain objects that calls forth our imagination.[7]

The movie-projector understanding of imagination assumes people, places, and things passively receive the images projected onto them; however, the Van Gogh painting was obviously not a blank canvas. Van Gogh's style and choice of colours induced a particular imaginative experience. The projection was not just one way. I projected onto the painting while simultaneously the painting projected itself onto me. The imagined painting was not the optical picture on the laptop screen but a co-creation between what was given on the screen and what I brought to the screen—a liminal or in-between space that does not fit into the common assumption of imagination somehow being inside us and projected onto the world. As the late maverick psychiatrist R. D. Laing wrote:

> This distinction between outer and inner . . . is a distinction between different modalities of experience, namely, perception (as outer) in contrast to imagination, etc. (as inner). But perception, imagination, phantasy, reverie, dreams, memory are simply different modalities of experience, none more "inner" or "outer" than any others.[8]

Imagination is neither entirely inner or outer. The imagined Van Gogh was imbued with both subjective and objective aspects. It was neither a mechanical reproduction of screen pixels or an entirely subjective "image in the mind" but a co-creation that arose in between the subjective and objective polarities of experience. This is why it is not possible to arrive at any one, single, objective, and true impression of a painting. No two people will see the painting in exactly the same manner. Another viewer might have felt a melancholy loneliness in the sparsely furnished room. Still another might have felt a wonky, skewwhiff disorientation in the not-quite-square room. There is always a subjective pole to imagining that filters what we perceive. And yet to brush aside the objective pole and claim a one-sidedly "inner" or entirely "fantasy" imagining goes too far, as David Abram writes:

> All of this could be brushed aside as imaginary distortion or hallucinatory fantasy if such active participation were

not the very structure of perception, if the creative interplay of the senses in the things they encounter was not
our sole way of linking ourselves to those things and letting the things weave themselves into our experience.[9]

The idea that we can easily separate the imagined from the so-
called "real" is not supported by the experiential evidence. A purely
objective stance, according to James Hillman, is just not possible
because "experience is never raw or brute; it is always constructed
by images".[10] In other words, not just paintings but all experience
is imbued with an imaginal component. As the novelist Philip
Pullman puts it:

You won't understand anything about imagination until
you realize that it's not about making things up; it's about
perception.[11]

Imagination is woven into all perception. In this regard, James
Hillman writes of imagination as a primary faculty: "In the beginning is the image: first imagination, then perception . . . we are indeed such stuff as dreams are made on."[12] In this understanding,
perceptions are not facts that point to material objects but malleable impressions, one of many ways in which we can imagine
self and world. As Jungian therapist Mary Watkins puts it, imagination "does not simply represent the given . . . but creates or
brings something new into being".[13] Images hover in an elusive liminal zone in between self and world, neither entirely a physical object "out there" in the world nor entirely an "inner" object within.

And yet, the common-sense assumption of imagination as an
inner realm or place is difficult to let go. In part, this is due to the
structure of language and the hold it has over basic understanding
and experience. Imagination as a common noun (a person, place,
or thing) suggests something to see, a place to go, or a thing to
hold. But imaginative experience is none of these. Images are not
things. As James Hillman writes:

> We never seem to catch imagination operating on its own, and we never can circumscribe its place, because it works through, behind, within, upon, below our faculties.[14]

Imagination is not just one faculty among others. It is not confined to any single skill area, such as visual sensation, memory, or creative thinking. What characterizes imagination from the sensory, emotional, cognitive, and intuitive is that it is found within all these faculties and brings them together without being subsumed by any of them. Images are seen, heard, felt, thought, remembered, and intuited.

The imagined Van Gogh was not just a visual image. All the senses were involved: both the physical senses and their imaginal equivalents. The physical sight that attended to the screen evoked an imaginal seeing, hearing, and feeling. The table, chair, and bed were seen with the eyes of imagination. The swish of the foliage outside the window was heard with the ears of imagination, as too was the cooling breeze felt with the touch of imagination. Imagined sights and sounds evoked imagined feelings and thoughts. The room had a certain vibe and mood. It got me thinking about who lived there and when they might return. And all of these imagined sensations, feelings, and thoughts were dependent on memories that on a very basic level allowed me to recognize "chair" and "table", and on a more subtle level, imbued the painting with intuitions about the kind of person who lived there. Imagination cannot be properly understood or approached in isolation. As Roberto Assagioli writes,

> Imagination is a function which in itself is to some extent synthetic, since imagination can operate at several levels concurrently: those of sensation, feeling, thinking, and intuition.[15]

Imagination brings together a synthesis of all the various psychological faculties, but imagination itself is neither a discrete faculty nor some kind of interior realm. So what exactly is it?

My description and reflection upon looking at the Van Gogh painting have proceeded far enough for me to now offer a tentative working definition of imagining as "the perception of images arising in between self and world". In other words, everything is imagined. Reality is imaginal. A perhaps bold claim that provokes a number of questions: *Surely, everything can't just be made up and imagined? Don't we need some kind of reality check? Isn't there a difference between fact and fiction?* These are understandable and important questions that will now take us into the difference between imagination and fantasy.

Imagination and Fantasy

An understanding of imagination as everyday perception is not to naively suggest that all imaginings are equally valid. While different perceptions of a Van Gogh painting are perhaps of little consequence, how we imagine ourselves and the world certainly does matter. For instance, to habitually imagine friends, partners, and therapists as disappointing, critical figures, despite available evidence to the contrary, is to be trapped within a single story of self and world, an imagining where the subjective pole of experience does not align with the objective, otherwise known as "fantasy imagining", a basic definition of which is given by the Jungian dream therapist Robert Bosnak:

> A mental process, akin to rational thinking . . . an indirect, disembodied feeling of distance, and a controlling, grasping attitude of habitual consciousness . . . the endless reconfirmation of pre-existing notions . . . erecting a wall against the fresh.[16]

Fantasy is a disembodied imagining in which the subjective cache of memories and beliefs operates largely unchecked by the evidence of the objective world. It is an imagination withdrawn from the world and stuffed inside; hence, the cliché of being "in your head" as a description for a fantasy life of frustrated desires, trapped within the confines of the known, unable to reimagine and adapt to changing circumstances. This requires a lot of effort to maintain, an effort we can call "neurosis", or psychological suffering, the result of alienating modern lifestyles and an education system that neglects the training of feeling and sensation. It is the rump imagination that remains when, through neglect or fear, sensory contact with lived experience is diminished, as James Hillman writes:

> The moment you leave sensing out of imagining, it is imagining that becomes an inferior function: sheer fantasy, mere imaginings, only a dream.[17]

This is not to suggest that fantasy imagining is a black-and-white issue or that sufficient sensory awareness will be able to create a true or entirely accurate imagining. Fantasy is always a matter of degree. A purely objective non-fantasy imagining is not possible. The subjective aspect of imagination can only be refined but never eradicated completely.

The image-centric approach sketched out in these pages is therefore focused upon what is required to enhance the process of how self and world come together in imagination: the cultivation of an embodied imaginal sensitivity that is malleable and able to move in accordance with the shifting sensory impressions that constitute the people, places, and things of the surrounding world.

Dictionary Definition: Inner Imagination

Fantasy imagining is so common that it has become synonymous with the dictionary definition of an entirely mental, or inner, imagining quite separate from the objective pole of sensed experience.

One standard dictionary definition of imagination states that it is "the act or power of forming a mental image of something not present to the senses".[18] Another states that to imagine is to form "pictures in your mind" of people, places and things "you have not experienced".[19] In this dictionary view, imagination is a mental or psychological interiority, a bit like the photo folder on a smartphone, a subjective cache of inner images quite separate from the everyday objective world. At best this inner imagination is treated as a creative faculty, "the ability to think of new ideas".[20] However, when these inner imaginings are projected onto the world, such as when a child imagines a tiny fish circling a goldfish bowl as "lonely", this is considered to be a subjective distortion of correct sensory experience, a pejorative "imaginary" or "fantasy" notion. The loneliness of the goldfish is seen to belong to the child's imagination not the fish; only those perceptions that accurately correspond to the factual real world "out there" are deemed to be valid.[21] However, as we have seen, this separation of imagination from sensory experience is itself a fantasy understanding, one that does not match the complexity of actual imaginative experience.

Inner Imagination: Four Limitations

The inner imagination definition is best understood as a metaphor rather than an actual description of what happens when we imagine. Images are only "as if" but not really inside us in the way photographs are inside a smartphone. To imagine a lonely fish is not necessarily a one-sided projection, as if pressing the SHARE icon and sending a digital photograph out into the world. Imagination is only "as if" an inner world, not an actual inner place or realm easily separated out from normal everyday experience. However, with overuse and a lack of alternative ideas, the difference between this inner imagination theory and actual experience can be easily missed.

A good example of this conflation between theory and experience is the popular concept of Subpersonalities.[22] Based on the assumptions of an inner imagination, "subpersonalities" are the idea that the imaginal people found in dreams, memories, and fantasies are symbolic representations of different aspects or parts of the personality. An angry figure in a dream might be considered a Boss subpersonality, as might a frightened child figure become a Child subpersonality.

The danger of this idea is that it can obscure the actual experience of imaginal persons, whether in a sleeping dream, a waking dream, a memory, fantasy, movie, or novel—which is one of meeting a person with the same individuality, consciousness, and intention as normal people in everyday life. It is only when we wake up from the dream, think about the memory, or leave the cinema that we have the afterthought of these characters as subpersonalities (for example, *Ah, yeah, the Brad Pitt character is my Hero subpersonality*).

Robert Bosnak describes the idea of subpersonalities as "a meta-psychological culture-specific afterthought, not necessarily related to observed phenomena".[23] The idea of subpersonalities is a simplification of a rich and complex imaginative encounter into a neat psychological theory. That's fine as far as it goes; theories help us step back and gain perspective. However, stepping back pushes us towards a rational thinking-about images that eclipses the quality of attention needed for imagining. As the following four limitations show, inner imagination assumptions are poorly aligned to what image-based therapists most value in experiential work.

Dualistic

The inner imagination assumes a dualism of inner and outer. Images have a proper location within and an improper projection onto the world, the limitation of which can lead to a preoccupation with a withdrawal of projections. In extreme cases of fantastical delusions, this may have some merit; however, in less disturbed individuals (that is, most people) the attempt to fit the complexity of imaginative experience into neat inner/outer categories is rarely satisfactory or clear-cut. As we have seen, images are neither entirely inner or outer; they arise in between self and world. Time and energy put into wondering about where images have come from, to whom they belong, and whether or not they are projections to be withdrawn to a source within is perhaps interesting, but needs to be recognized as a rational thinking-about images at odds with the commonly understood importance of experiential work in psychological transformation.

Rationalistic

The rationalistic limitation of an inner imagination understanding is alive and well in those people in art galleries who spend more time reading embossed rectangles of explanatory blurb than looking at paintings. The blurb gives a quick hit of understanding. It informs about the historical period, the painter's style and influences, and so forth, but knowing what a painting "means" in this way is not why most people go to an art gallery. They want to feel taken out of their everyday worries and transported, if only for a few moments, into the imagined world of the painting and painter, all of which could happen if they only spent more time actually attending to the painting instead of reading the blurb.

In the same way that art gallery blurb about a painting is obviously not the same as the imagined painting, so too inner imagination ideas such as Subpersonalities or the Inner Child are not the same as a lived encounter with an imaginal person. For example, a Witch subpersonality is an idea of a generic witch, a representation of spooky feelings and taboo thoughts, all of which creates an abstracted distance from the up-close imaginative encounter with the edgy presence of an autonomous witch-like figure. As an after-the-event reflecting back, this might have a place, but during waking dreams and active imagination, talk of "subpersonalities" and "inner parts" is an unnecessary undermining of imaginal perception, a movement from a felt engagement with images to a rational thinking-about images that is once again at odds with an experiential approach.

Narcissistic

Inner imagination obviously focuses attention inwards: images are assumed to be personal and subjective, perhaps even something we have made up and have a certain control over. The danger is that it leads to a narcissistic self-absorption, in which the ego becomes identified as "the-person-doing-the-imagining", a distortion that serves to further bolster and suit the needs of this egoic identity, moving away from the more relational imaginative engagement that might challenge egoic identification.

Mechanistic

Inner imagination theories of change are mechanistic. Imagination is inside, and we are somehow on the outside peering in, like a mechanic working on a car engine. The images inside this machine imagination are theorized "as if" mechanical "objects" or "parts", and imaginative change is the moving around of these image objects. For example, an image can move from unconscious into conscious awareness, such as when a memory bubbles to the surface; an image can be projected onto the world, such as when we fall in love with an idealized figure; or a new image can be placed within, as happens with the memories of everyday events or through visualization practices. However, notice how nothing new is created in this understanding. Imagination is a zero-sum game, a collection of imaginal components that can be moved around but never increased or destroyed. This notion offers little to support therapists in further understanding how imagination seems to create new ideas, identities, and ways of being, a process that rarely proceeds in a linear, predictable, and controllable mechanical fashion.

The inner imagination definition is at best a partial understanding, ill-suited to the needs of psychotherapeutic work. What we shall be developing in this book is a much closer match between theory and practice, an understanding aligned to the complexity of imagining and its place in psychotherapy and everyday life. It is an understanding that points towards the quality of imaginal perception itself rather than thinking-about images, a joined-up imagination that brings self and world together not further apart, and a theory of change that embraces the human irregularity of dreams rather than the fantasy of a mechanical imagining.

We have now made a start in establishing a working definition of imagination as "the perception of images arising in between self and world". In the next chapter, the first of the Waking Dream chapters, this theoretical ground is used as a basis to explore the practical and experiential considerations needed to cultivate an embodied imagination.

1. Vybarr Cregan-Reid, *Footnotes: How Running Makes Us Human* (London: Ebury Publishing, 2017), 1.

2. Robert Bosnak, *Embodiment: Creative Imagination in Medicine, Art and Travel* (Abbingdon, Oxon.: Routledge, 2007), 70.

3. John Berger, *Ways of Seeing* (London: Penguin Press, 2008), 10.

4. Nathan Schwartz-Salant, *The Borderline Personality: Vision and Healing* (Asheville, NC: Chiron Publications, 1989), 176.

5. David Abram, *The Spell of the Sensuous* (New York: Vintage Books, 1997), 58.

6. James Hillman, "Image-Sense", in *Working with Images: The Theoretical Base of Archetypal Psychology*, ed. Benjamin Sells (Thompson, CT: Spring Publications, 2000), 171.

7. David Abram, *Becoming Animal: An Earthly Cosmology* (New York: Penguin Random House, 2011), 32.

8. https://selfdefinition.org/psychology/R-D-Laing-the-Politics-of-Experience-chapter-one.pdf

9. David Abram, *The Spell of the Sensuous* (New York: Vintage Books, 1997), 130.

10. James Hillman, *Re-Visioning Psychology* (New York: Harper Perennial, 1992), 177.

11. Philip Pullman, *The Secret Commonwealth: The Book of Dust, Volume Two* (London: Penguin, 2020).

12. James Hillman, *Re-Visioning Psychology* (New York: Harper Perennial, 1992), 23.

13. Mary Watkins, *Invisible Guests* (Thompson, CT: Spring Publications, 2000), 68.

14. James Hillman, "Image-Sense", in *Working with Images: The Theoretical Base of Archetypal Psychology*, ed. Benjamin Sells (Thompson, CT: Spring Publications, 2000), 175.

15. Roberto Assagioli, *Psychosynthesis: A Manual of Principles and Techniques*, (London: Thorsons, 1993), 143.

16. Robert Bosnak, *Embodiment: Creative Imagination in Medicine, Art and Travel* (Abbingdon, Oxon.: Routledge, 2007), 76.

17. James Hillman, "Image-Sense", *Working With Images: The Theoretical Base of Archetypal Psychology*, ed. Benjamin Sells (Thompson, CT: Spring Publications, 2000), 183.

18. https://www.merriam-webster.com/dictionary/imagination

19. https://www.collinsdictionary.com/dictionary/english/imagination

20. https://dictionary.cambridge.org/dictionary/english/imagination

21. James Philips and James Morley, ed. *Imagination and its Pathologies* (Cambridge, MA: The MIT Press, 2003), 40.

22. John Rowan, *Subpersonalities: The People inside Us* (Abbingdon, Oxon.: Routledge, 1990).

23. Robert Bosnak, *Embodiment: Creative Imagination in Medicine, Art and Travel* (Abbingdon, Oxon.: Routledge, 2007), 16.

Chapter 2

Waking Dreams No. 1 – Entering

> Imagination is first provoked and infused by the earthly place where we dwell.
>
> —David Abram[1]

Everyone is imaginative. To imagine is an innate ability that can be enhanced with the appropriate care and attention. What creates the belief of not being an imaginative person is usually the assumption that imagining is a kind of alternate realm separated from normal everyday life—a fantastical, three-dimensional, virtual reality with dancing dolphins in surround-sound stereo—only available to special "creative types".

But this view only directs attention away from discovering a realistic experiential understanding of what it actually means to imagine, a crucial first step towards recovering and enhancing imaginative life. This first in the series of Waking Dream chapters, therefore, begins with a clarification of the quality of imaginal perception needed to enter a waking dream—both the conventional "eyes-closed" variety and the novel "eyes-wide-open" application in generic psychotherapy and everyday life.

The Hypnagogic State

The psychological term for imaginal perception in a waking dream is a Hypnagogic State. Derived from the Greek *hypnos* (sleep) and *agogeus* (guide) it was coined in the early 19th century by French psychologist L.F. Alfred Maury during his studies on wakefulness within the dream state, such as can happen spontaneously for a few moments, either upon falling asleep or waking up, when there is the awareness of being in a dreamscape alongside a recognition that we are also safely tucked up in bed.[2]

In a normal dream there is only a single awareness, one of being in a dreamworld that convinces us entirely that it is the only reality; whereas, in the hypnagogic state of a waking dream, there is a dual awareness where, as the Jungian therapist Robert Bosnak writes, "you participate in two equally true realities simultaneously: the world that is imagined and [the physical world]".[3]

The hypnagogic state is the quality of perception that occurs in the overlap of imagined and physical realities, a threshold consciousness in between waking and dreaming, hence a "waking dream". A hypnagogic overlap of imaginal and physical that we can see in the working definition, established in chapter 1, of imagination as "the perception of images arising in between self and world". To imagine is synonymous with the in-between overlap of the imaginal and physical.

My viewing of *The Bedroom* painting by Van Gogh, which I used in chapter 1 to illustrate this imaginal perception, is an example of being in a hypnagogic state: the imagined world of the painting coexisted alongside an awareness of it as a physical image on a laptop screen in the same way that a dreamworld can coexist or overlap with an awareness of lying in a physical-world bed. To view a painting is not to disappear into the single awareness of an entirely imagined alternate reality, like the scene in *Mary Poppins* where they jump into the pavement chalk painting. The imagined world of *The Bedroom* with its cooling breeze passing through the green-tinged window overlapped with an awareness of street-traffic noises coming through my physical world window.

Viewing a painting is just one example; all the arts are hypnagogic. The imagined reality conjured by a photograph, movie, or novel overlaps with the physically sensed reality of the photographic print, movie screen, or text. When a long-forgotten song is played on the kitchen radio (physical reality) and takes me back in time to the events of a teenage summer romance (imagined reality) this is again a hypnagogic state, an evocation of memory that is a key component of any psychotherapy, in which the events of the past (imagined reality) overlap with the awareness of sitting on a comfy chair opposite a therapist (physical reality).

Indeed, how a client perceives a therapist—the story they tell themselves about the therapist's thoughts and feelings and life beyond the consulting room—is an imagined reality that overlaps with the posture, gestures, facial expression, and tone of voice in the physically sensed therapist. In all these ways and more, the hypnagogic state can be seen in everyday life. All we need do is learn to notice and let it grow.

The practice of waking dreams is one way to notice the hypnagogic state. While spontaneous waking dreams on the threshold of sleep usually don't last very long, the practical conditions and skills needed for an extended exploration can be cultivated.

We begin to do this in the following exercise exploring the hypnagogic state present in any memory. The aim is to give an experiential taste of this subtle imaginal perception by remembering your bedroom, or any other place whose details can be easily recalled. The instructions build up a 360-degree assemblage of imaginal details, as a writer might describe a scene in a novel. In order to avoid drifting off into a daydream, the sensations of breathing are used to maintain the hypnagogic overlap between the physical breathing body in the present and the imaginal memories from the past. I suggest you read through the instructions and then first do the exercise as an "eyes-closed" waking dream. With practice, you will be able to sustain an increased imaginal awareness for longer periods that will carry over into "eyes-wide-open" waking dreams.

Exercise 2.1: Waking Dream Memory

Sit comfortably in a quiet place where you will not be disturbed.

Spend a few moments attending to the physical sensations of breathing: the rise and fall of your chest; how long or short each breath is; the slight pause between each breath.

Continue to follow your breathing as you now also imagine standing in your bedroom, looking out the window.

Notice what you see through the window: any objects or movements that attract your attention, the quality of the light, the weather.

Notice how near or far away things are.

Allow your breath to help you focus.

Notice any sounds and how warm or cold it is to stand beside the window.

Allow the colours, shapes, textures, and sounds to become ever clearer.

Tune in to the atmosphere of your bedroom window. How it feels to be there.

Now very slowly, imagine turning to face into the bedroom.

Notice any items that particularly attract your attention in the room; whether the bed is made or unmade; whether the door to the hallway is open or closed; any sounds or smells.

Allow your breath to help you focus on the images.

Allow the colours, shapes, textures, and sounds to become ever clearer as you simultaneously notice your feelings and thoughts about the bedroom.

Take your time and finish the exercise when you are ready.

Literalism, Fantasy, and the Hypnagogic

If imagination is synonymous with the hypnagogic state, then the opposite is also true: an impoverished imagination is an absence of the hypnagogic, an absence that can go painfully wrong in one of either two directions—literalism or fantasy.

Literalism, in the sense of there only being a literal world of observable facts, is the most obvious absence of an imaginal sensibility. Things are simply as they are, fixed and immutable objects. A famous example is given by Charles Darwin in his autobiography, in which he describes the loss in later life of the enjoyment of the arts he experienced as a young man:

> I have tried lately to read Shakespeare, and found it so intolerably dull that it nauseated me. I have also almost lost my taste for pictures or music.... My mind seems to have become a kind of machine for grinding general laws out of large collections of facts.... The loss of these tastes is a loss of happiness, and may possibly be injurious to the intellect, and more probably to the moral character.[4]

The ability to become easily absorbed in the story-world of a play, once simply taken for granted, had become a struggle or impossibility. To only have the text of Shakespeare, the canvas of a painting, or the physical impressions of music without the rich imaginal background they once evoked is a painful loss; it spills over into the surface images of everyday life, which become equally flat, dull, and lifeless, no longer able to move and inspire us into reverie, story, and creative possibility. However, this does not mean that imagining has entirely disappeared. As the Wallace Stevens poem "Metaphors of a Magnifico" goes:

> Twenty men crossing a bridge
> Into a village
> Are twenty men crossing twenty bridges
> Into twenty villages[5]

There is always an imaginative background. Each person who crosses a bridge into a village will have a more or less unique imaginal perception. How the local person notices and feels about the village will be different to that of a tourist, as will that of a pensioner differ from a teenager and that of a religious fundamentalist from a dispassionate empirical scientist.

As James Hillman puts it, even the literal-minded perception of "fact, reality, science" is itself an imaginal perception that we "no longer see as a myth"[6]. The issue with literalism is not so much that imagination has entirely gone; it is that the imaginal has become conflated with the physical. Instead of a hypnagogic overlap of imaginal and physical, the two are fused into a single consciousness, an overly objective imagining of a single, matter-of-fact world.

Fantasy imagining is a loss of the hypnagogic in the opposite direction to literalism. As described fully in chapter 1, fantasy is an overly subjective imagining, out-of-touch with the immediacy of sensed experience, a habitual reconfirmation of pre-existing beliefs that makes it difficult to learn and adapt with changing circumstances, a fantasy imagining that makes it all too easy to slip into a story world. The issue is not a *lack* but a *surfeit* of imaginal ability, and the disconnection of these images from a physical basis in the world, a disembodied imagining in which there is little or no overlap between imaginal and physical. Once again, this is a single consciousness, like literalism, but one that is trapped within the imaginal rather than the physical.

Entering a Waking Dream: The Three Steps

The entry into a waking dream is all about the establishment of the hypnagogic state: navigating a tension between literalism and fantasy. The more literal-minded will need to cultivate imagining alongside physical perception, as in exercise 2.1 between the recollected bedroom and the physical breath. Those more prone to the flighty wanderings of fantasy will need to cultivate an embodied attention that stabilizes and connects imagining with the physical.

The following three steps describe the practical principles required to cultivate the hypnagogic. Note that this is not intended as a formulaic technique to create any particular image content; whatever shape or direction a waking dream takes is only secondary. The primary focus in these steps is creating the conditions needed to enter into and maintain a process of imagining.

Step 1: Imaginal Sensations

The first step is to emphasize a sensory imaginal attention towards the surrounding image environment. Due to habitual overdependence on sight, visual images will usually predominate at first; however, it is important to also include auditory, tactile, olfactory (smell), gustatory (taste), and vestibular (movement) images. In this way a total sense response is established, as in exercise 2.1, in which the visual images of the bedroom (bed, door, window, light, time of day, and so on) were complemented with auditory images (the sounds outside the window and inside the building), tactile images (the temperature of the room), olfactory and gustatory images (perhaps the stale air in the bedroom and the aroma of toast coming from down the hallway), as well as vestibular images (*Now turn very slowly*).

It is important to recognize that the sensory attention of embodied imagination is not an exclusively inner felt sensation. Sensation does not merely reside inside the body. Sight, hearing, and touch also connect us to colours, sounds, and textures in the surrounding world. Embodied imagining, therefore, balances attention between the subjective and objective poles of experience, creating a sense of inhabiting an encompassing image environment. For instance, in exercise 2.1, the imagined sound of a radio would have drawn attention to the open bedroom doorway and the hallway beyond.

Step 2: Imaginal Feelings and Thoughts

The second step includes feeling and thinking responses towards the image environment. Often these spontaneously emerge as the imaginal scene becomes more fully sensed in step 1: the mood of the scene imbues itself into our feeling state as we look around and think about our surroundings. However, the introduction of feeling and thinking responses can push the balance of experience towards the subjective pole, collapsing the tension needed to maintain the hypnagogic state. In order to avoid this, it is important to distinguish between two types of responses: analytical and imaginal.

Analytical responses are ideas and feelings about the imagery. For example: *What does the old woman in the bed mean? What part of my character does she represent? Oh no, it's not all about my mother again is it?* Such responses move away from immediate imaginal experience into interpretations and associations, taking us outside the process of imagining, as described in chapter 1. This results in an overemphasis on the subjective pole of experience at the expense of the objective, collapsing the required balance needed to maintain the hypnagogic state. For this reason, analytical responses that arise during a waking dream are simply ignored.

The synthetic nature of imagination, also described in chapter 1, is one that includes all the psychological faculties, including thinking and feeling. While analytical responses are avoided, the type of thinking and feeling we do want to include are imaginal responses: those directly evoked from within the process of imagining. For instance: *I like this bedroom. It feels good here. I think the person under the bedclothes is my partner, but I'm not entirely sure. Who is that singing along to the radio in the kitchen?* In the same way that step 1 combined a subjective "felt sense" with a corresponding sensed object, so too do these imaginal feeling and thought responses connect to imagined objects, maintaining the balance of attention between self and image-world needed for the hypnagogic state. For this reason, imaginal responses are actively sought and included.

Step 3: Imaginal Sensations, Feelings, and Thoughts

Steps 1 and 2 are introduced sequentially for practical purposes. The initial focus in step 1 on embodied imagining is easier if feelings and thoughts are temporarily ignored, as at this stage they will most often be analytical responses.

Once a sensual awareness of the imaginal scene is established, the imaginal feeling and thought responses of step 2 will naturally emerge. However, once we have worked through these two steps, we can see that imaginal sensations, feelings, and thoughts are only artificially separated. In step 3, we therefore work to bring together a synthesis of imaginal sensations, feelings, and thoughts. For example: we contemplate the rain outside the window while feeling the cosy wellness of being indoors; or we look at the old woman in the bed while thinking about what we want to say; or we listen to the commotion erupting down the hallway while noticing the growing knot of tension in our stomach.

Entering Waking Dreams in Everyday Life

The best place to first cultivate waking dream skills is in "eyes-wide-open" everyday life practice. The surrounding sights and sounds are simply there, in a way that they are not in "eyes-closed" practice, when constant effort is needed to maintain the hypnagogic state. All we need do is get outside and look, listen, and touch. This is an important basis to cultivate for all waking dream work, as sense-based awareness is often diminished in modern life, where so much time is spent in static, temperature-controlled, indoor spaces, in front of screen-based work and entertainments.

To the extent that sunlight, wind, and rain pass unnoticed, as a kind of background wallpaper to a busy life, the same will happen in eyes-closed waking dreams, resulting in a waking dream that feels forced and made up—a disembodied, mental idea about sunlight, wind, and rain. In the following "eyes-wide-open" exercise, we will take advantage of the increased stimulation and possibility of the unexpected in an outdoors environment as a means to cultivate embodied imagining.

Exercise 2.2: Waking Dream Walk

Step outside and move slowly.

Take your time. Breathe.

Notice what you find interesting: an object or a place; a river or a rain cloud.

Stop in a place or beside an object of interest. If nothing in-particular stands out, just pick somewhere.

Step 1: Imaginal Sensations

What shapes, colours, and shading do you notice?

What sounds, smells and textures?

Be as open as possible to what is before you.

Step 2: Imaginal Feelings and Thoughts

How does it feel?

Savour your felt response for a while, however strong or subtle.

Notice also any thoughts, ideas, words, or conversations.

Breathe.

Step 3: Imaginal Sensations, Feelings, and Thoughts

Allow sensory attention and feeling/thinking response to come together.

Attend. Respond. Attend and Respond.

Take your time.

Finish the exercise, or move on to another place, and repeat.

Entry Points

The opening scene in a waking dream is called an "entry point", a narrative scenario that will best allow for the initial establishment of the hypnagogic state. What makes for a good entry point is a benign scene without any dramatic tension, such as the bedroom scene in exercise 2.1; more dramatic scenes, involving some kind of threat or challenge, evoke a strong feeling and thinking response, which will eclipse the sensory attention to the surrounding image environment needed for "Imaginal Sensations" in step 1. Dramatic scenarios can be explored, as we will discuss in chapter 4, but only after the hypnagogic state has been firmly established within the safety of the entry point. Here we consider the relative merits of three types of entry point: generic, bespoke, and spontaneous.

Generic Entry Points

Generic entry points are off-the-shelf options found in books on guided imagery, visualization, and active imagination. Popular examples include: a meadow, the mouth of a cave, or the foot of a mountain path, often with further instructions for the development of the waking dream, with obstacles to overcome and destinations to achieve. The advantage of the clear direction offered by these entry points, especially for beginners to waking dream work, is that it avoids wasting energy trying to decide what imagery to initially focus upon; however, there are a couple of disadvantages to generic entry points to be aware of.

First, while most people will have a benign response to the suggested meadow, cave, or mountain path, there will always be someone who has difficult associations with the prescribed imagery. At best, this results in time spent processing difficult experiences rather than imagining new ones during the waking dream; at worst, the unanticipated strength of feeling and thinking undermines the safety required to establish the hypnagogic state. Second, any entry point is merely a stage upon which a drama will unfold, but imagining generic scenes, especially if this continues beyond the entry point, can divert attention from the spontaneously unfolding process of imagining, which is the beating heart of any waking dream drama.

Bespoke Entry Points

Bespoke entry points are chosen from the current imaginal life of the waking dreamer. Example scenes include:

- a memory (as in exercise 2.1)

- a dream
- a previous waking dream
- a movie
- a novel.

The advantage of these entry points is the specificity of detail offered. The familiarity of an everyday scene or memory will support the fine-grained attention to sensory details needed to establish the hypnagogic state. Scenes from dreams, movies, or novels are also applicable here, although being entirely imagined can make them slightly more challenging than familiar physical places.

The important point once again is that whatever scene is chosen needs to feel like a safe place. If there is a dramatic scene that we would like to explore, it is best to choose an entry point either before or after this tension-filled moment. Once the hypnagogic state is established, we can then move forward or backwards through the waking dream to explore the more challenging scenes, as we shall see in chapter 4.

Spontaneous Entry Points

Spontaneous entry points emerge from the stream of images constantly bubbling away at the edges of awareness. The uncertainty of this approach can be a little unnerving; however, the clear advantage is that it involves an imaginal scene taken from directly within the spontaneously unfolding process of imagining. In this way, it skips past the "empty stage" setting and dives straight into a drama that more directly reflects the current psychological life of the waking dreamer than is possible when using generic or bespoke entry points.

The practical consideration of a spontaneous entry point is not what imagery is chosen but that a clear decision is made to pick a scene from the choices available. Only by choosing to focus upon one scene will it be possible to clarify the sensory detail needed to establish the hypnagogic state. It can be easy to delay this choice and become distracted by waiting for a particularly significant image to emerge. However, the content of what is imagined is not what is important in this choice. While the bread section in a supermarket might not seem like a promising entry point, in the same way that all roads once led to Rome, so too any one image will take us into a process of imagining, as we shall soon see in the following transcript example.

Entering Waking Dreams in Psychotherapy

Daphne is a fictional client, a composite of my work with many people, whose progress we will follow through these Waking Dream chapters. A woman in her early thirties, Daphne's life seemed to be going well: successful career, nice flat, lovely husband. She came to see me for psychotherapy shortly after her marriage because anxiety and depression had begun to gnaw away at her normally upbeat, optimistic personality.

Here, we meet Daphne some 15 minutes into her sixth therapy session, struggling to articulate concerns about a recent decision to find a new job. I suggested a waking dream as a way to explore these concerns. This first part of the transcript demonstrates finding a spontaneous entry point and then working through the three entering steps. I am the therapist Th: and Daphne is the client Cl:.

Th: So, when you are ready, close your eyes.

Cl: Okay.

Th: First of all become aware of your breath and the process of your breathing through your body . . . notice how long or short each breath is . . . how fast or slow.

Cl: Okay.

Th: Follow the breath down on the in-breath, and let it help you tune in to how you're feeling . . . the mood and atmosphere you have within your body, without needing to label or explain . . . just breathe in to how you feel.

Cl: Yeah, I'm all wound up inside. There is a tension in my arms and legs. It's the anxiety.

[Once the waking body and feeling awareness was established, I then made a start on the waking dream.]

Th: Now, following the breath down on the in-breath, let it help you to enter into a landscape of imagination . . . breathe alongside the images passing through your mind . . . just take your time . . . and when you are ready let me know what you see.

[Step 1 began with an invitation to describe the imaginal scene.]

Cl: I'm not really seeing anything, just random changing colours.

Th: That's alright. Sometimes it takes a bit of time. Just keep breathing, and tell me when anything does appear.

[Lack of coherence should not be seen as a setback, and in my tone, I tried to convey confidence that something would emerge in due course.]

Cl: *[Pause]* It's hard to describe—a kind of cushion? But also, I'm seeing a supermarket shelf: the bread section. And also trees: a summer forest.

Th: Lots of imagery coming through now. Take your time, and pick one image, the one that stands out most clearly, the one of most interest to you now.

[As no particular image stood out, I simply invited Daphne to choose one. It is the process of imagining that is important, not any particular content of imagining.]

Cl: The cushion image, that one.

Th: Okay. Can you tell me more about the cushion?

Cl: It's sort of a meringue colour, a blob shape.

Th: A meringue blob shape. Okay. Can you stay focused on that? Keep watching, and see what other details emerge.

[*It is important not to give up too quickly on a vague or abstract image. Here, I worked to stimulate an interest that would allow more detailed imagining to emerge.*]

Cl: [*Pause*]. It's the back of a chair. Yes, I'm looking at the back of a chair.

Th: The back of a chair.

[*This simple reflection back to Daphne served multiple purposes: it confirmed I was listening; reinforced a focus upon the image scene; and in a nondirective fashion invited Daphne into further description.*]

Cl: Like on an airplane.

Th: Like an airplane chair. How far away are you from the chair?

[*Asking about distances helps establish an awareness of the waking dream as an encompassing three-dimensional image environment.*]

Cl: It's right in front of me. I'm on an airplane.

Th: You are on an airplane.

Cl: Yes, I'm sitting on an airplane, the window seat. I can see the wing and fields below, some wispy clouds.

Th: What kind of seat is it? What's the texture and feel of it?

Cl: It's leather or some kind of leather substitute. Grey and very comfy—a big wide seat.

Th: What else can you see around you? How big is the cabin?

[*Open questions gather more descriptive detail.*]

Cl: It's a small plane, only a dozen or so rows. Not many people on board, five or six.

Th: And what can you hear in the cabin?

[Here I began to include imaginal senses other than the visual.]

Cl: Just engine hum . . . oh, and the ping of an air steward call button . . . and I can sense people moving around at the back of the cabin . . . I can hear glasses clinking, like stewards preparing drinks.

Th: And can you detect any movement in the airplane?

Cl: Yes! It's a little bumpy—not bumpy, more a vibration through the chair. We are in flight.

Th: Bumpy, a vibration. Okay. And is there a place in your body where you feel that most clearly?

Cl: *[pause]* Yeah, through the chair, but more in my feet, under my feet—a tiny constant vibration.

Th: A tiny constant vibration.

Cl: Yeah, it's got a sort of rhythm, a beat—*Da Da Da Daa*—over and over.

Th: And what's the temperature in the cabin?

Cl: Pleasant.

Th: And what does it smell like?

Cl: Like a new car smell. Nice. I like it.

Th: And how does it feel to be there?

[As the last two responses from Daphne had touched upon feelings ("Pleasant" and "I like it"), I followed her lead and moved into entering step 2.]

Cl: Pleasant: I'm relaxed, like I'm being looked after.

Th: You feel looked after.

Cl: Yes, I feel kind of privileged.

Th: Can you stay with that feeling for a moment [*pause to give her time*]. Can you say more about that feeling?

Cl: It reminds me of how I feel when I go on holiday, that carefree feeling. It happened last summer quite strongly, I was so pleased to get away. We flew to Rome.

[*The invitation to "Stay with that feeling" took Daphne too strongly into the subjective pole of experience, the effect of which was to move her away from the waking dream imagery. Perhaps this had been an unnecessary intervention, as the feeling state had already been mentioned twice.*]

Th: Just stay with the imagery. You are on the airplane. The seat is wide and comfortable. It feels carefree and privileged.

[*I simply ignored the comments from outside the waking dream and returned Daphne to the imaginal scene in the present tense, moving into entering step 3 by combining imaginal body with feeling response.*]

Cl: Yes. I love it. I'm so relaxed here.

Th: Feel the rhythm in your feet as you look again at the seat back in front of you [*pause to give her time*], and also feel the more subtle vibration through the chair as you look again out the window at the wing and relax into that sense of being carefree and looked after [*pause*].

[*Unlike the first two entering steps, which are invitations to describe the imagery, this third step is more of an active direction or instruction.*]

Th: What is happening now?

Cl: The vibration is kind of soothing, and I'm just looking out the window at the wing.

[The entry point was established, to be continued in the next chapter, where we will begin to see how the unfolding imagery reflects Daphne's everyday life.]

The Therapist Role and Parallel Imagery

In psychotherapy, waking dreams constitute a collaboration between therapist and client—both parties are involved, and the imagery is not a private perception only available to the client. In the same way that images appear between a reader and the pages of a novel, so too do images appear between the therapist (the reader) and the verbal description of the waking dream given by the client (the novel). This is called "parallel imagery", as it will be similar but not exactly the same as what the client imagines. While parallel imagery is not shared directly with the client the quality of this imaginal perception by the therapist will be important in three respects:

1 In paying attention to parallel imagery, the therapist is "imagining with" rather than "thinking about" the client and their waking dream journey—a walking-the-talk stance that will create a supportive atmosphere and build trust in the waking dream experience for the client.

2 Parallel imagery informs therapist interventions from within the process of imagining; for example, a vaguely imagined scene will be apparent from the parallel imagery, and the therapist will invite further description from the client to add detail and specificity. If the therapist is only thinking about the client's waking dream description, interventions will likely come from outside the process of imagining, which can jar the client out of the hypnagogic state; for example, "What part of you is that a representation of?"

3 Maintaining awareness of parallel imagery that is not the same as the client's prevents the therapist from unwittingly sharing images, imaginal feeling, and thinking responses that are alien to the client's waking dream. For example:

Cl: The cabin is bumping up and down with turbulence. The seatbelt signs have pinged on.

Th: How do you feel about this frightening situation?

Cl: I'm not frightened about the turbulence.

Notice how the fear of turbulence was not reported by the client directly but rather, assumed by the therapist. While this client felt assertive enough to correct the therapist, this is nevertheless an interruption to the waking dream that is best avoided. An even worse scenario occurs when a less confident client adopts the therapist's imagery. Each time such a difference is left uncorrected, the waking dream moves further away from the client's spontaneously arising imagery, a topsy-turvy case of the client following the therapist rather than vice-versa.

Exercise 2.3: Waking Dream Self-Practice

A therapist is not an essential requirement for waking dream work. However, the difficulty of self-practice is that without prompts from a therapist it can be all too easy to lose focus and drift into unconscious daydreaming. To avoid this, we can replicate aspects of the therapeutic role by recording the waking dream as it happens. Instead of voicing a description to a therapist, we can write, type, or use a voice recorder to capture what we see, hear, touch, and so on, as well as imaginal feeling/thinking responses. With practice, we can learn to do so without opening our eyes, minimizing the possibilities for distraction. An added bonus is having a record of the waking dream to read or listen to afterwards.

1. David Abram, *Becoming Animal: An Earthly Cosmology* (New York: Penguin Random House, 2011), 268.

2. Gary Lachman, *Lost Knowledge of the Imagination* (Edinburgh, Scotland: Floris Books, 2017), 96.

3. Robert Bosnak, *A Little Course In Dreams* (Berkeley, CA: Shambhala, 1986), 44.

4. http://www.victorianweb.org/science/darwin/reading.html

5. http://poets.org/poem/metaphors-magnifico

6. James Hillman, *We've had a hundred years of psychotherapy and the world's getting worse* (New York: Harper Perennial, 1992), 17-18.

Chapter 3

Immersive Imagination

An image is a place, an environment in which we find ourselves.

—Robert Bosnak[1]

Since we can know only fantasy images directly and immediately, and from these images create our worlds and call them realities, we live in a world that is neither "inner" nor "outer".

—James Hillman[2]

Some say the world is a "vale of tears"; I say it is a place of soul-making.

—John Keats[3]

Imagination creates whole worlds. Images are places. The viewing of the Van Gogh painting described in chapter 1 began with a flat screen, but it did not end there. What started out as a two-dimensional, pixelated painting on a laptop ended up as a three-dimensional imaginal environment. Imagination took me beyond what was immediately presented until it was as-if I was actually there, inside the sparsely furnished bedroom, so much so that I even worried about someone coming back and discovering me nosing around.

Of course, the physical everyday world did not completely vanish. The laptop and desk it sat on had simply moved to the edges of my awareness, as happens at the cinema when the story world of a movie becomes foreground and the plush seats and popcorn munching of the theatre recede into the background. The ability to become absorbed and transported into an imaginal landscape turns the conventional inner imagination view inside out: instead of images being inside us, it is we who find ourselves within imagination. It is a reversal that raises several interesting questions: *Hey, that might be all well and good in art galleries and cinemas, but surely you are not suggesting we walk around in this dreamy fashion all the time? Isn't that just a self-absorbed fantasy delusion? Don't we need to stand back and see what is really there?*

The conventional view does not like to think of normal everyday life as an imagined one. Imagination is meant to be a discrete faculty that can be turned on and off, to be used in the appropriate settings and then abandoned in favour of "standing back" and "seeing what is really there". In this second theoretical chapter, I continue to critique this conventional understanding by introducing an "immersive" aspect of imagining alongside the creative dimension of imagination as the ability to conceive of new possibilities.

The Imagined World

To walk down any street is an effortless immersion within a fully imagined world. The surrounding image environment appears without any conscious effort to "stand back" and "see what is really there". Spindly dark lines in the middle distance, a pale blue expanse overhead, and a nearby translucence are instantaneously narrated into a street story with trees, blue skies, and shop windows.

It does not matter that the trees are seen in profile in the middle distance. We do not perceive two-dimensional trees and say to ourselves in wonder, *How odd!* Imagination goes beyond what is immediately given and presents us with three-dimensional imagined trees. Similarly, it does not matter that the sky is partially obscured by these trees. We do not philosophize as to whether an unseen sky exists or not; imagination fills in this sensory gap, and we imagine a seamless continuation of sky beyond the trees. Nor does it matter that the coffee shop window is dimly lit; we do not leave this darkness as an existential emptiness—imagination pictures an interiority of tables and chairs, staff and customers, music and chatter.

In this way the sights and sounds of the everyday world are stitched together with feeling, thinking, and sensation into an immersive story world. Despite the concerns of the inner imagination view, we do indeed walk around in a dreamy fashion all the time, as Shakespeare acknowledged when he declared: "We are such stuff as dreams are made on."[4] Everyday reality is an imagined one. Immersive imagining is not something that can be turned on and off. It is the story-fabric construction of the world, as the Jungian therapist Robert Romanyshyn writes:

> Between subject and object a story appears, which is expressed in a way of seeing and of speaking about the world. The story which appears is the appearance of psychological life.[5]

This definition of a psychological life, which appears "between subject and object" as "a way of seeing" and "story", is a close match to the definition, presented in chapter I, of imagination as "the perception of images arising in between self and world". It is a meeting of the psychological and the imaginal first recognized in modern times by Carl Jung, who wrote that "Image is psyche" and "Every psychic process is an image and imagining,"[6] an equivalence of imaginal and psychological that the post-Jungian James Hillman developed into a foundational assumption of image-centric psychology:

> . . . a psychology that starts neither in the physiology of the brain, the structure of language, the organisation of society, nor the analysis of behaviour, but in the processes of imagination.[7]

We are always imagining. Whether in memories of the past, present-moment perceptions of the world, or fantasies about the future, there is no getting away from the primacy of images in all actions, feelings, and thoughts. All of human social, economic, scientific, or religious life is an immersive imagining derived from psychic images. It is the raw datum of psychological life and, therefore, the beginning, middle, and end point of any image-centric therapy. This perspective opens a large conceptual space for the cultivation of imaginative life, one that requires taking a step back to consider something of the historical context of this image-as-psyche idea.

Ideas have a history and the psychological has, over time, come to mean something other than what it originally meant. The concern of modern psychology with mental states, perhaps located in the brain, certainly in an individual person, and a focus upon inner feelings, thoughts, and images is a relatively recent invention. The original meaning of the Greek word *psyche* was not "mind" or "mental", which derive from another Greek word, *menos*, but was originally understood in relation to three root meanings, each of which points to a connection with imagination: breath, butterfly, and soul.[8]

First, *psyche* as "breath" suggests a sensual process of mutual exchange circulating between self and world, similar to the embodied imagination described in chapter 1. Second, psyche as "butterfly" connotes a delicate, fragile, and fleeting nature, not easily captured or pinned down, similar to the emphasis we have been placing upon imagination as a continual process, a dynamic quality of perception rather than a fixed or static imaginal content. Third, *psyche* as "soul" requires a little more unpacking, but will most clearly demonstrate the link to imagination.

The Jungian conception of soul, used interchangeably with psyche, is again not a modern one. The perhaps conventional notion of soul as a personal spiritual essence, an invisible homunculus somehow living inside the mind, is once again a relatively recent invention. In pre-modern times soul was not an inner entity but understood as an in-between zone of porous exchange that connected the interior self to the external world.[9] Here soul named a subtlety of experience that was neither entirely inner or outer, subjective or objective, but instead belonged to a third category that conjoined self and world, as indeed can still be recognised in contemporary usage when we talk of a "soulful" moment, meal, conversation or walk in the country, where the soulfulness is not just inside us but arises by way of interaction with people, places and things.

The image-centric psychology developed by James Hillman focuses upon differentiating this middle ground of soul arising in between self and world as the realm of images and imagining. It constitutes an imaginal experience that is difficult to describe due to modern languages having lost the necessary vocabulary for something that is neither a subject nor an object. This is why psychological literature generally avoids defining soul and imagination, either assuming them to be part of an inner world or alluding to a mystery too sacred to define.

James Hillman avoids both these pitfalls in sketching out the characteristics of this in-between soul as:

- a middle-ground between us and events, doer and deed
- a viewpoint towards things rather than a thing itself
- a perspective rather than a substance
- a deepening of events into experiences
- that unknown component that makes meaning possible
- the imaginative possibility in our natures—that mode that recognizes all realities as primarily symbolic or metaphorical.[10]

From the standpoint of soul, the everyday world is truly an imagined one. Soul is a psychological in-breath and out-breath that moves in the middle-ground between us and events; it is neither a thing nor a substance, yet is inseparable from all feeling, thinking and sensation. Soul is the imaginative possibility in our natures that combines sense experience with memory to create a narrative understanding, noted in our working definition of imagination as "the perception of images arising in between self and world". The complete eradication of this imagining by "standing back" and "seeing what is really there" is the impossible fantasy of a literal world entirely separated from subjective influence. It would be to walk down a street like a scientist holding up a test tube to the light, a self-conscious and questioning stance towards the most basic sensory experiences.

This is not to suggest that all imaginings are equally valid; the concern with self-absorbed fantasy is a genuine one, even if the solution of eradicating all imagining is not. Imagination can and often does go wrong. In all manner of ways, misperceptions of self and world are a source of psychological suffering: anxious fantasies that never materialize, self-doubts that hold us back, and relationships that endlessly recycle the same old arguments. How we imagine the world clearly matters.

Habitual Reimagining

Image-centric therapy understands psychological suffering in respect to the limitations of fantasy imagining, as described in chapter 1. Here, we consider further how fantasy is a habitual reimagining of self and world.

In simple and familiar situations, the habitual reimagining of the world makes sense. Indeed, a degree of habituation is to be expected. To be human is to become familiar with particular places, people, and tasks. Habits allow us to leave an art gallery and walk down any street without having to put time and energy into understanding anew every passing tree, cloud, and coffee shop window. Without this habituation, the beauty of the world would overwhelm us. Without habits, we would step outside each morning and spend the whole day awestruck by the mystery of trees, lost in the fascination of cloud patterns, and entranced by reflections in shop windows. However, the cost of this efficiency is a trade-off with wonder. As the novelist Anthony Doerr writes,

> The easier an experience, or the more entrenched, or the more familiar, the fainter our sensation of it becomes. This is true of chocolate and marriages and hometowns and narrative structures. Complexities wane, miracles become unremarkable, and if we're not careful, pretty soon we're gazing out at our lives as if through a burlap sack.[11]

Habitual reimagining maintains the expected by filtering out the novel, strange, and unfamiliar. The danger in this is that it can lead to a life without curiosity, possibility, and new meaning, a forever ordinary dullness rather than enchanted interest—also known as being depressed. This is why people go to art galleries in the first place: to find inspiration that goes beyond habitual attitudes, interests, and concerns; a portal into a brighter existence, an enlivened imagining coloured and flavoured by the thinking and feeling of a Van Gogh, Monet, or Velazquez; an imagining that will hopefully not stop when they leave the art gallery but carry over into everyday life, as an enhanced sense of being there with the dog walkers, traffic lights, and rain drops snaking down the window pane on the bus home, a sense of participation and involvement that is the very antidote to the alienation and isolation characteristic of psychological suffering.

Soul-Making and Novel Images

Image-centric therapy is a journey or movement away from the limitations of habitual reimagining. Whether it takes place in an art gallery, a walk in the park, or a psychotherapy session, it is the engagement within a process of imagining that is seen to be healing and transformative. It provides a framework for psychological health that guides therapeutic work towards the cultivation of an ever more fluid and adaptable imaginative life, an engagement in the activity of images in everyday life that James Hillman names "soul-making":

> The making of soul-stuff calls for dreaming, fantasying, imagining. To live psychologically means to imagine things; to be in touch with soul means to live in sensuous connection with fantasy. To be in soul is to experience the fantasy in all realities and the basic reality of fantasy.[12]

Soul-making breaks up the story-fabric of the habitually imagined world. It makes conscious the assumptions of fantasy imagination and contemplates new possibilities and meanings, a re-visioning of the routine such that clouds, coffee shops, and even saying hello become fresh and new all over again, initiated by what I shall be calling "novel images": figural or stand-out perceptions that bring the process of imagining into conscious awareness.

Love affairs and divorces, births and bereavements, new jobs and job losses—any significant life event can become a novel image. To walk along a beach and watch a sunset is to be moved by a novel image. To view a painting, read a book, or talk with a psychotherapist is to be taken on a journey by novel images.

Take for example the first photographs of Earth from space, in which the pale blue oceans and wispy atmosphere of our planet against the emptiness of space were a revelation. Never again would it be quite so easy to assume a vast world divided into discrete nation states and people. A more accurate and complex imagining crept into the zeitgeist: a comprehension of shared life on a tiny and fragile planet.

Now incorporated into collective understanding these historic images of planet Earth have inevitably lost much of their initial novelty value. New images from the margins of the normal are where we find today's novelty: space buggies travelling across the surface of Mars, glacier ice cliffs crashing into the arctic sea, blazing forest fires, riots, protests—anything that arrests attention and interrupts a business-as-usual imagining.

Wherever novel images appear, the effect will be the above-mentioned "deepening of events into experiences" that is soul. What before was simply an ordinary and unnoticed event is turned into a lived experience that touches and moves us, often with an element of anxiety or excitement, a dramatic tension that demands to be resolved.

A simple everyday example might be when we are walking down a street and something out of place catches our eye (*What could it be?*). The enigmatic thing is too far away to make out clearly. There is no easy comprehension. No quickly joined-up imagining as happens with "tree" and "coffee shop". A gap remains between self and world, a middle ground where the now conscious process of imagining flips and wriggles around, seeking a best-fit picture and story (*Is it a police crime scene, a rough sleeper's tent, an alien spaceship?*). Upon closer inspection none of these fantasies are supported. The enhanced, up-close, sensory information allows a moment of recognition (*Ah, that's what it is then—just a fluorescent shopping bag caught up in the railings*).

The dramatic tension is resolved as the world comes back together again, and yet, this is not a complete return to business-as-usual. Immersive imagining has returned in a slightly expanded sense that now incorporates the novel image, and it is the navigation of this interruption and enhanced return of immersive imagining in response to novel images that is soul-making.

Creative Imagination

Novel images open up the middle ground between self and world. The previously taken for granted becomes noticed and felt (*Look at his eyes. He does care about this*). The assumed way of things becomes provisional and uncertain (*Maybe he's not so cold-hearted after all?*). To enter into this malleable, in-between imaginal perception is the primary creation of soul-making. As James Hillman writes, the focus of psychological creativity is "the awakening or engendering of soul".[13] The middle ground of soul is both a questioning of the old and also the creation of new possibilities from beyond the boundaries of habitual imagining (*What if I spoke to him about it. How might that be?*)

To notice and allow these possibilities to take shape and colour and feeling in imagination is a crucial step towards any form of creative action in the world. As therapist Rollo May writes: "Imagination is the home of intentionality."[14] Without the ability to imagine a future event or way of being as a realistic opportunity, it will be all too easy to revert to habitual imagining (*No, he'll take it the wrong way; best keep quiet*). In this way, hopes and dreams remain unrealized subjective fantasies about what could have been; whereas, if the uncertainty of the new can be tolerated, then imagined possibilities will lead to real-world actions and events (*"Hey, you know that thing that happened? . . ."*).

Image-centric therapy assists clients in noticing then following through on the creative possibilities offered by novel images. In the first instance, this will be the novel image that catalyzed entry into therapy. The troubling thoughts, feelings, or sensations the client is suffering will be related to their associated novel images: an obsession to the image of a beautiful work colleague; an anxiety to images of angry people and being angry; a migraine to fantasies of being criticized. Within this work, the therapist will be on the lookout for further, smaller-scale novel images, as described by therapist Chris Robertson:

> The craft entails listening for that change of tone (a dis-cordant harmony), the unfinished sentence, the pregnant pause, what is unsaid but felt as emergent. The quality of trust that you will be heard can catalyze the courage to risk speaking these "missing" possibilities.[15]

Sooner or later, a crack in the story-fabric of immersive imag-ining will open upon another world of "missing possibilities": an atypical moment in the content or style of the client's narrative, facial expression, gesture, or some other out-of-character be-haviour that transforms the session into the middle-ground of soul-making. Here, the therapeutic task is to provide the care and attention that allows these missing stories to be further explored in imagination: an image-centric approach to psychological suffer-ing and its transformation, the practical strategies of which we continue to explore in the following Waking Dream chapter.

1. Robert Bosnak, *Embodiment: Creative Imagination in Medicine, Art and Travel* (Abbingdon, Oxon.: Routledge, 2007), 9.

2. James Hillman, *Re-Visioning Psychology* (New York: Harper Perennial, 1992), 23.

3. John Keats, personal correspondence, April 1819.

4. William Shakespeare, *The Tempest*, act 4, scene 1, line 148.

5. Robert Romanyshyn, *Psychological Life: From Science to Metaphor* (Milton Keynes: The Open University Press, 1982), 16.

6. Benjamin Sells, ed. *Working With Images: The Theoretical Base of Archetypal Psychology* (Thompson, CT: Spring Publications, 2000), 5.

7. James Hillman, *Re-Visioning Psychology* (New York: Harper Perennial, 1992), xvii.

8. Guy Dargert, *The Snake in the Clinic: Psychotherapy's Role in Medicine and Healing* (London: Karnac, 2016), 2.

9. Richard Tarnas, *Cosmos and Psyche: Intimations of a New World View* (New York: Plume/Penguin Group, 2007), 16.

10. James Hillman, *Re-Visioning Psychology* (New York: Harper Perennial, 1992), xvi.

11. Anthony Doerr, *Four Seasons in Rome: On Twins, Insomnia and the Biggest Funeral in the History of the World* (New York: Scribner, 2008), 54.

12. James Hillman, *Re-Visioning Psychology* (New York: Harper Perennial, 1992), 23.

13. James Hillman, *The Myth of Analysis* (New York: Harper Perennial, 1972), 21.

14. Rollo May, *Love and Will* (New York: W.W.Norton & Company, 2007), 211.

15. Chris Robertson, *Transformation in Troubled Times: Re-Vision's Soulful Approach to Therapeutic Work* (Forres, Scotland: TransPersonal Press, 2018), 101.

Chapter 4

Waking Dreams No. 2 — Exploring

Imagination is the home of intentionality.

—Rollo May[1]

The most we can do is dream the myth onward.

—Carl Jung[2]

The landscape in the books I read were to me not merely
landscapes more vividly portrayed in my imagination . . .
they seemed to me . . . to be actually part of nature itself,
and worthy to be studied and explored.

—Marcel Proust[3]

To explore a waking dream is to follow the mysterious and strange.
Sooner or later, a novel image will emerge in the shape of a peculiar situation or event—perhaps an enigmatic smile across a dimly lit bar or a quirky yellow bird snoring on a fence post, something that confounds expectations and provokes curiosity.

The effect of a novel image will be a slight pause in the pace of the unfolding imagery, a pause within which we consider the possibilities for action. Do we smile back or move down the bar? Do we creep past the snoring bird or wake it up with a clap? How we choose to respond will be the impetuous that moves the waking dream forward. Each step will be a movement away from the initial safety of the entry point, a journey beyond the limitations of habitual imagining into an ever more expansive and adaptable imaginative life.

This second in the series of Waking Dream chapters draws upon the context of immersive imagination, as presented in the previous chapter, to present the principles and practices that allow us to move, act, and explore the imaginative terrain of a waking dream. We begin with a breakdown of these imaginal movements into three steps before going on to offer strategies, examples, and exercises for both "eyes-wide-open" and "eyes-closed" waking dream exploration.

Exploring a Waking Dream: The Three Steps

Step 1: Novelty

Once the hypnagogic state is established at the entry point, as described in chapter 2, the first step towards exploring the waking dream is to notice novel images. Sometimes novel images will stand out and impinge clearly upon attention, but not always. This is for a couple of reasons: first, due to unrealistic expectations of only bold novel images diverting attention away from noticing more subtle novel images at the margins of awareness, or second, the entry point itself is a novel image that is not done with us just yet—perhaps we are sitting on a beach enjoying a sunset, and it feels good, so why leave?

In either case, all we need do is continue with the three steps of entering, dwelling upon the imaginal sensations, feelings, and thoughts within the entry point scene. In time, a new novel image will emerge.

Step 2: Possibility

The second step considers the possibilities created by the novel image. By attending to imaginal responses towards the novel image, the details of possible future actions emerge and clarify, such as getting up from lying on the beach and investigating a nearby rock pool. However, if possibilities fail to emerge, and all we want to do is remain still and do nothing, this is probably due to the strength of difficult feeling evoked by the novel image.

If this is the case, there are two options: first, emphasize sensory imaginal attention towards the surrounding image environment (as in step 1), which can balance the feeling response, or second, restart the waking dream from a safer entry point, where there may be more tolerable novel images that will allow greater confidence in the initial exploration.

Step 3: Activity

The third step is to put the imagined possibilities into action: actually get up and move towards the rock pool. The important consideration in this step is to avoid any rushed movements (as in exercise 2.1, "turn very slowly"). If we move too quickly, the pace of the unfolding imagery can bypass the attention to sensory detail needed to maintain the hypnagogic state.

A careful handling of step 3 therefore resists what Robert Bosnak calls "the natural impulse of the imagination to rush forward"[4]. The action is slowed down by treating the result of each movement as a new entry-point scene, where the three entering steps are repeated. For example, once the client has moved from lying on the beach to standing up, this new upright position is treated as an entry-point scene, working through the imaginal sensations, feelings, and thoughts of the entering steps. Once the hypnagogic state has become re-established in this new scene, only then do we look out for another novel image, reflect on possibilities, and take action. In this way, the waking dream moves forward by looping back and forth between the entering and exploring steps.

Exploring Waking Dreams in Everyday Life

The three steps of exploring describe a process that operates hundreds of times a day. Imaginal signals in the environment are constantly informing decisions on where to go and what to do. Billboards, bridges, and skyscrapers can be novel images that evoke feelings, thoughts, and actions. Each time we get on a bus or train carriage it is a sensitivity to the surrounding image environment that informs where we decide to sit or stand and when to get off.

The following exercise explores any nearby street, garden, or park as an "eyes-wide-open" waking dream by working through the three steps: noticing novel images, considering possibilities, and taking action.

Exercise 4.1: Exploring a Landscape

Step 1: Novel Image

Step outside and look around.

Take your time.

Notice how you feel drawn here and not there.

How something, big or small, is attracting your attention.

Whatever stands out, go there.

Attend to it with all your senses.

What shapes, colours, and shading do you notice. What sounds, smells, and textures?

Savour your feeling response, however strong or subtle.

Also notice any thoughts, ideas, or words.

Breathe.

Step 2: Imagining Possibilities

What action would feel satisfying?

What expression would feel like a good thing to do?

Allow the details to take shape and clarify in imagination.

Do you want to move closer? Walk around? Reach out and touch?

Do you want to dance, wave, or make a crazy gesture?

Breathe.

Step 3: Activity

Now carry out the action.

Do it slowly.

Notice what changes occur.

Attend to what you now see, hear, smell, and so on.

Savour your feeling and thought responses.

Breathe.

Finish the exercise, or allow another novel image to emerge and repeat.

Exploring Waking Dreams in Psychotherapy

The following transcript continues from where we left off in the "entering" chapter, with my client Daphne Cl: well established in the hypnagogic state at the entry-point scene, a window seat on an airplane. Recollect that the immediate context for starting the waking dream was her anxiety about finding a new job. In this next exploring section, as soon as Daphne is invited to notice any novel images (step 1) something of this everyday anxiety emerges in the waking dream, creating a strong feeling that threatens the hypnagogic state.

The transcript shows how I worked as the therapist Th: to re-cover the waking dream by increasing imaginal attention on the surrounding imagery before moving into a consideration of possibilities for exploration (step 2). Once a clear intention is described Daphne is then guided into acting it out (step 3).

> Th: As you look around what stands out for you? What is most interesting?
>
> [*The exploration began with step 1: looking for novel images.*]
>
> Cl: The veneer mahogany interior.
>
> Th: What does it look like?
>
> Cl: It's very shiny. It runs all around the lower half of the

cabin. Oh, my gosh, it's a private jet! It's quite small. Like the ones you see in movies!

[*I could not help making the connection between the private jet and the earlier mention of a privileged feeling (in chapter 2), but I managed to avoid sharing this analytical thinking-about response.*]

Th: Is there anything else catching your attention?

[*The focus remained on describing the novel image.*]

Cl: Yes! The other passengers are very well dressed, like business people. No one is talking. It's a subdued atmosphere.

Th: A subdued atmosphere.

Cl: [*Pause*] It feels like there's been a mistake. I can't afford this kind of ticket. I'm not meant to be here.

Th: It doesn't feel relaxing anymore?

Cl: No, not anymore. It's a bit stressful. Someone is going to find me out. [*Pause*]. It's like how I feel about the jobs I'm applying for: a nice idea, but not for me, people exposing the errors in my applications, interviewers laughing at me behind my back when I leave.

[*The strength of feeling out of place had taken Daphne away from the waking dream.*]

Th: Can you focus on the imagery. What is happening on the airplane? What do you notice?

[*I simply ignored her associations with everyday life and refocused attention on the image environment to recover the hypnagogic state.*]

Cl: [*pause*] It's really swish. I never noticed properly before. The leg room is huge. The carpet is really thick [pause]. I can still hear the clinking glasses behind me . . . and some voices.

[The tone of "some voices" suggested a new novel image.]

Th: Can you hear the voices?

Cl: Not clearly, but they are not far away. A light conversational tone—people that know each other well, probably the air stewards.

Th: Not far away, behind you. How far?

[Distances help maintain the waking dream as a three-dimensional image environment.]

Cl: Yeah, not far—three metres maybe.

[I waited for more description but nothing came.]

Th: Okay. Can you keep sensing into the comfort of the leather seat and the deep carpet *[pause]*. Keep listening to the conversation behind you *[pause]* in this private jet where you feel you are not meant to be.

[I was careful here to reintroduce the dramatic tension of "private jet" alongside the imagery of the cabin.]

Cl: Okay.

Th: *[pause]* Is there anything you would like to do now?

[Step 2: Considering the possibilities for exploration.]

Cl: I'm not sure.

Th: Okay. Take your time *(pause)*. Notice what is attracting your attention. What you are curious about?

Cl: The voices.

Th: Can you tell me about them.

Cl: Chit-chat, friendly.

Th: So, you are sitting in your plush seat, in this small jet with the mahogany veneer, listening to this friendly chit chat behind you. What might feel like a good thing to do right now?

Cl: I think I'd like to turn around.

Th: Okay, why don't you do that? Take your time. Make sure to move nice and slow [*pause*] and then when you are ready tell me what you see.

[*Step 3: Action, the outcome of which is then approached as a new entry-point scene by working through the three entering steps, describing the air stewards and the imaginal feeling and thinking responses towards them.*]

Eyes Closed or Eyes Wide Open?

The advantage of an "eyes-closed" waking dream is the focused attention on the imaginal environment allowed for by the removal of visual distractions in the physical environment. However, there are a couple of significant disadvantages to "eyes-closed" waking dreams for some psychotherapy clients that are important to recognize and avoid.

First, the invitation to "close your eyes" can place an unhelpful pressure on clients to imagine on demand, a self-consciousness that can interrupt rather than enhance the flow of the therapy session, fostering either a frozen inability to get an image or the forced, made-up feeling of a self-invented waking dream, both of which are why many therapists and clients often give up on waking dream practice altogether.

Second, the "eyes-closed" approach can exacerbate a tendency towards fantasy imagining in those clients with a so-called "overactive" imagination, due to unwittingly overemphasizing the subjective pole of experience. This is why conventional therapeutic approaches "contraindicate" (recommend avoiding) image-based work for such clients, particularly those at the borderline and psychotic end of the pathology spectrum.

Any such blanket avoidance of image work rests upon the faulty assumption of imagination as a discrete psychological faculty that can be ignored in favour of a strictly cognitive, emotional, or body-based approach. As described in chapter 3, the images presented in memories, in-the-moment perceptions, and future fantasies are the raw material of all therapeutic work. There is no getting away from the place of imagination in psychotherapy.

In this view, any exacerbation of fantasy imagining is not due to the waking dreams per se but their particular "eyes-closed" application for some clients. As long as the safety of the entry-point scene is carefully considered, avoiding unduly traumatic memories, then an image-centric approach can be continued with all clients by treating generic psychotherapy work as an ongoing "eyes-wide-open" waking dream.

An "eyes-wide-open" waking dream avoids therapy getting in the way of the therapy. The adjustment towards an image-centric approach is more subtle than an explicit invitation to "close your eyes" with no obvious break in the session to interrupt the flow of the client's imagining. A bypassing of any undue attention on the therapeutic strategy avoids provoking resistance to imagining in those more anxiety-prone and perfectionistic clients, and for those clients with a so-called "overactive" imaginations, the continued visual contact with the therapist and physical environment helps avoid an overly subjective flight into fantasy. Furthermore, beyond an avoidance of the above-mentioned disadvantages an "eyes-wide-open" approach is also an important means to carry over the imaginal perception of waking dreams into an experiential awareness of the activity of images in everyday life.

"Eyes-Wide-Open" Entry and Exploration

Multiple opportunities spontaneously arise in generic psychotherapy sessions for "eyes-wide-open" waking dreams. The hypnagogic state is always present to some extent in the overlap between the consulting room and imagined scenes within client memories, future fantasies, and in-the-moment perceptions of the therapist and whatever else is noticed and commented upon (furniture, décor, ornaments, paintings, lighting, passing street noises, and so on). When any one of these scenes stands out for whatever reason (repetition, strong emotional charge, therapist's intuition, and so on), it can be taken as an entry point into an "eyes-wide-open" waking dream.

Here, an image-centric approach will emphasize a fulsome experiential description of the imagery by first applying the three entering steps (imaginal sensations; imaginal feeling and thinking; and imaginal sensations, feeling, and thinking) before moving on to the three exploring steps (novelty, possibility, activity). While a sustained exploration similar to an "eyes-closed" waking dream is possible, a shorter exploration is more often the case with the "eyes-wide-open" approach.

What will establish and maintain the "eyes-wide-open" experience is the understanding that a waking dream is a series of "now" moments; in other words, it happens in the present tense. Both past and future tenses create a once-removed perspective from outside the process of imagining; therefore, entry points in memories or future fantasies must be adjusted into a present-tense description. Similarly, entry points from in-the-moment perceptions will need to be maintained in the present tense. In the following three examples the key therapist interventions for each of the entering and exploring steps are given, with the adjustments into a present tense imagining highlighted in bold:

Memories and Future Fantasies

The entry point is established by first switching the past-tense memory ("My mother-in-law came to visit") or future-tense fantasy ("My mother-in-law is going to visit") into the present tense. The least invasive strategy is to switch therapeutic interventions into the present tense; that is, "**How is it** to have her visit?" rather than "How was/will it be it to have her visit?", or reflecting back "**It is** embarrassing" rather than "It was/might be embarrassing".

This will often need to be repeated a few times before the client catches on and follows the therapist's lead into a present-tense waking dream exploration; however, if the client continues in the past tense, a more explicit switch can be suggested: "How about we get back in touch with how that was by stepping into the memory **as-if it is happening right now**"? Whichever route into the present tense is taken will involve working through the entering and exploring steps. For example:

Entering

Step 1: "Tell me where you **are** when you meet your mother-in-law. How big **is** the room? What **is** she wearing? How **do you** greet her? How far **do you** stand from her? How **does she** look at you? **What is** her facial expression?"

Step 2: "How **do you feel** as she looks at you like that? **What is** going through your mind?"

Step 3: "Okay, feel the embarrassment **as you stand there beside her.**"

Exploring

Step 1: "What stands out most **as you meet her**? What **do you notice** about her most strongly?"

Step 2: "What would you like to do?"

Step 3: "Okay, try that **now**."

Instead of figuring out why the mother-in-law is so difficult, the client is given the opportunity to process the feeling responses evoked and to experiment with novel actions.

The Transference

How the client imagines the therapist is called the "transference". When transference is strong or frequently recurring, it is conventionally taken as a rich vein for therapeutic attention, indicative of the client's wider relational style and history.

However, it can be all too easy for a therapist to skip past the opportunities for experiential work by refuting the transference ("I'm not at all angry with you") and moving quickly into an analytical thinking-about approach; for example, by tracing the origins of the transference in childhood relationships ("Who is it that I am reminding you of at the moment?" or "Who are you really angry with?").

Instead, an "eyes-wide-open" waking dream approach is one that avoids this reality-checking move by accepting the transference as an entry-point scene and then exploring the feelings, thoughts, and action-impulses within the imaginal perception of the therapist. This is a strategy that will meet and maintain the session within the present tense by always bringing the focus back to what is happening in the now; for example, if the client offers "You kind of remind me of my father," then the therapist would respond, "What is it about me that is familiar?" rather than "Tell me more about your father," which would move off further into history.

The below example of working through the entering and exploring steps begins when a client pauses and looks directly at the therapist and says, "I sometimes think it would be cool if we could be friends. I think we'd get on":

Entering

Step 1: "You imagine we'd get on. What **is it** about me that makes you say that?"

Step 2: "How does that make you feel, **being here with me**?" and then "What thoughts go with that feeling of safety?"

Step 3: "Okay, so **as you sit here now**, with me sitting back in my chair, relaxed, and speaking in this soft, gentle voice, **you fee**l looked after and cared for."

Exploring

Step 1: "And is there anything in particular that suggests my friend potential?"

Step 2: "How does that make you feel, **as you share that with me now**? What thoughts are going through your mind about it? What would else would you like to share with me?"

Step 3: [The sharing of the feelings and thoughts and future fantasies is the action step.]

Objects

A consulting room filled with paintings and wall coverings, ornaments and statues, soft toys and play figures will entice imaginative process out into the open. Environmental factors such as buzzing flies, fresh-paint smells, babies heard crying through a wall, and sudden bursts of sunshine through a window can all become novel images for imaginative attention, as will happen most readily for ecotherapists working outdoors (see also exercises 2.2 and 4.1).

An image-centric approach will assume that which has particularly drawn client attention in this way is not a random distraction but reflective of a psychological life that can be further explored as an "eyes-wide-open" waking dream. The following example outlines the entering and exploring steps in response to a client's sudden and sustained interest in a dusty old teddy bear:

Entering

Step 1: "Tell me about Teddy Bear. How is she sitting? And what kind of expression **does she have**? Where **is** she looking?"

Step 2: "**How do you feel** towards Teddy Bear?" and then "**What are you** wondering about her?"

Step 3: "Take a moment and allow yourself to really feel the bittersweet feeling **as you look at** Teddy Bear over there in the corner of the room."

Exploring

Step 1: "What in particular **draws your attention** towards Teddy Bear? What stands out for you about her?"

Step 2: "Is there anything you feel like doing?"

Step 3: "Okay, go ahead and pick her up."

The Therapist Role and Pacing

How frequently a therapist asks questions and offers reflections is an important consideration in the facilitation of a waking dream. Too frequent interventions can be a distraction for the client. If insufficient time is given to allow for an imaginal experience, the client will have little to report back and be in danger of making up answers to satisfy the overly zealous therapist rather than focusing on the actual waking dream imagery.

However, if too much time goes by without therapist support, the client will be in danger of drifting out of focus and slipping into the single consciousness of a daydream. A balance therefore needs to be found between too many and too few interventions. While the variety of waking dreams and dreamers means there are no easy rules to follow, pacing will be informed by tracking the following four information streams:

1 Client verbal report of waking dream.

2 Client nonverbal responses: breathing, facial expression, body movements, and gestures. (Note: it is best to glance occasionally, rather than continuously, as even with closed eyes, clients will sense and become distracted by a too-close visual attention from the therapist.)

3 Therapist attention to parallel waking dream imagery: sights, sounds, smells, and so on (as described fully in chapter 2).

4 Therapist imaginal feeling, thinking, and sensation responses to parallel waking dream imagery.

The pace of client verbal report will be the main factor. When it is frequent, the therapist will be alert to how fast the imagery is unfolding. If the imagery is unfolding nice and slowly, only occasional brief reflections and simple, open questions will be needed to direct the client through the various stages.

However, if the client is racing through the waking dream, the therapist will interrupt more frequently and ask for descriptive details that will serve to slow down the pace and better support the sensory attention to detail needed to maintain the hypnagogic state; for example: "Can you say more about that?" or the more explicit "Can we slow things down a bit and really look at this table?"

With less frequent verbal report from the client, it is much harder to gauge the pace of the unfolding imagery. Here a simple "What is happening now?" request will serve to both maintain client focus and keep the therapist in synch with the client, rather than asking about imagery that has not been mentioned for some time, which can pull the client out of the process of imagining.

Nonverbal client responses, such as a pronounced sigh or sudden shudder, will be an important indicator of the strength of feeling response to the waking dream. Here, it will be important to intervene and refocus on the surrounding imagery, rather than becoming overwhelmed by the feeling response and losing the hypnagogic state. With less physically demonstrative clients, the therapist will rely on their own strength-of-feeling responses to parallel imagery as an indicator for when to intervene in this regard.

1. Rollo May, *Love and Will* (New York: W.W.Norton & Company, 2007).

2. Carl Jung, *The Archetypes and the Collective Unconscious* (Collected Works, Vol. 9, Part I), 160.

3. Marcel Proust, *Remembrance of Things Past*, Vol 1 (London: Penguin Press, 1989), 93.

4. Robert Bosnak, *Tracks in the Wilderness of Dreaming: Exploring Interior Landscape Through Practical Dreamwork* (New York: Dell Publishing, 1996), 33.

Chapter 5

Animistic Imagination

Set aside the learned ways of perceiving the world as dead matter for your use, and see if you can recover again your actual perception of the world as a community of beings to whom you are meaningfully related.

—Erazim Kohak[1]

If we are willing to accept internal controls upon the imagination, we will have succumbed already in soul to the same authoritarianism that would dominate the body politic. The connection between submission to technical manipulation of imagination and submission to external controls is subtle, but it is real.

—James Hillman[2]

Animism is the attribution of human qualities and status to non-human creatures, places, and things. While the original coinage by Victorian anthropologists was a pejorative description of the spirit beliefs of so-called primitive people, in recent times animism has been having something of a renaissance.

A "new animism", removed from the distortions of these colonialist origins, has captured the interest of contemporary psychologists, philosophers, and scientists for the study of consciousness, ethics, and ecology.[3] It offers an emerging rehabilitation of animism that provides the context in this chapter for a discussion of the animistic aspect of imagination, which is to say, the inherent personifying tendency of imagining.

As we saw in chapter 1, even a Van Gogh painting with no human figures directly depicted was nevertheless filled with imaginal persons. The first was the missing occupant of the room, the person imagined to have only recently folded the covers of the bed and puffed up the pillows, a person who I worried might return and discover me nosing about, a state of unease exacerbated by the two portraits on the wall above the bed, personified as scowling with irritation at my unwelcome presence.

Perhaps this attribution of human qualities to non-human canvas is acceptable, but beyond the arts it can feel worrisome to grant a personhood to images. It goes against the grain of what we have learnt to be true. (*Isn't this animism just a tinkering with a primitive belief system, a regressive and childish embarrassment, possibly even a dangerous flirting with insanity?*)

Animistic imagination presents a challenge to the scientific belief in trees, rivers, and rocks as insensate, inanimate matter; however, as we shall soon see, this modern view is at best only a partial reflection of how we experience the world. In hidden nooks and crannies, animistic imagination is alive and well in everyday life, the most obvious example being the enchantment of childhood.

Childhood Animism

Imagine a broad Highland river with grey gravel banks, a summer evening stillness of trees. Imagine humid air, a steady murmur of wild water running out to sea. Imagine as if you are a child—a child crouched beside a tidal pool at the river's edge. Imagine your hand as it reaches out over the cool surface, a moving dark line. Imagine a tiny fish darting out from cover, appearing and disappearing amongst the algae-bearded rocks and weeds, a sustained moment of fascination. Imagine as the lonely fish cruises about in search of its brothers and sisters, wondering where they have all gone and how long it will take to find them.

I was that child by the rock pool. The story ends when my grandfather, fly fishing up-stream, sent his hook into my hair. I will never forget the sudden violence of that steel barb against my scalp; yet, I like to think the memory has remained with me for other reasons—as a reminder of how absorbed I was during those drawn-out damp moments; how the murk of weeds and the glide and hover of a fish once captured my whole attention; and how the animistic entry into the thinking and feeling of a tiny fish once felt like the most natural thing in the world.

Children just simply know how to extend imaginatively across the species barrier and converse with animals, plants, and places. Everything has a story path. A tree is lonely, a cloud is cold, and a stone wants to join its friends on the opposite side of a stream. As writer and wilderness advocate Jay Griffiths puts it:

> To a child, everything is lit with intent, following its story path, coursing with will. Ascribing a liveliness to the world brings the child's imagination alive; it refuses to allow either the world or the mind to be inert.[4]

Crouched on the gravel banks of a Highland stream, my childhood self did not ask what the tiny fish meant. It was not a symbol; it did not represent anything other than itself. I simply beheld the wonder of its mysterious being, an animistic imagining of a little fish person with brothers and sisters, hopes and fears, likes and dislikes, just like my own.

But childhood animism does not last. Acculturation into inanimate modernity begins early. Cute stories about lonely fish and sad clouds soon become frowned upon, then ignored, and finally dismissed outright as silly make-believe, a division of the world between real and unreal that ushers doubt into a child's imagination, a doubt exacerbated by the indoor confinement of the classroom, where sensual attention is directed away from puddles, clouds, and puppies towards the flatness of the page, whiteboard, and screen.

In this way, the animating magic is withdrawn from the surrounding world, no longer a perceptual interaction with trains, plastic action figures, and raindrops snaking down window panes. However, animistic imagining does not entirely disappear. As David Abram writes, animism in modern times has become specialized in reading:

> The "inert" letters on the page now speak to us . . . a form of animism that we take for granted, but it is animism nonetheless—as mysterious as a talking stone.[5]

It is an animistic imagining that we can perhaps trace back to the mysterious process of learning to read, when the slow running together of letters resulted in that delicious moment when an image would suddenly appear ("C . . . a . . . t: Cat!")

Of course, adulthood proficiency means the familiar letters and words no longer impinge upon us as they once did; we can now skim past the text and forget the page is speaking to us and conjuring a world of imagination, but hopefully, as you read these words, you will be aware that this book is not written by a robot. Something of my author personality and narrative voice will come across in my word choice and sentence construction—an imagined author personality, perhaps similar to the actual me, but really the result of imagination filling in the gaps between the words, a co-creation between reader and text that is no different to that of animistic childhood chat with plastic dolls and puppies.

Ancestral Animism

Ecopsychologist Theodore Roszak attributes childhood animistic imagining to an inheritance from the ancestral past, an "innate animism" regenerated anew by each generation "as if it were a gift, in the newborn's enchanted sense of the world".[6] The so-called primitive peoples Victorians labelled "animistic" were the remaining pockets of a culture that once spanned the globe. Indeed, for 99 percent of the history of humanity we have been animists, a way of being in the world that is arguably hard-wired into human DNA, a genetic imprint unchanged since the Stone Age, which finds brief expression in early childhood prior to adulthood acculturation into the modern world view.

Evidence of ancestral animism can be drawn from archaeology and anthropology.[7] The common characteristics of animism are discernible from post-medieval accounts, when Western explorers first moved out across the globe, as well as from recent studies of those indigenous cultures that have evaded modernity.[8]

In the famous phrase of the anthropologist Levy-Bruhl, animism is a *participation mystique*": an imaginative identification with other people, creatures, objects, and places in which human consciousness and intelligence are shared with all. Earth is not an inert thing or dead object but a living subject. As the cultural anthropologist Richard Nelson writes of animistic belief:

> A person moving through nature—however wild, remote, even desolate the place may be—is never truly alone. The surrounds are aware, sensate, personified. They feel. They can be offended. And they must, at every moment, be treated with the proper respect.[9]

Every rock face, river mouth, and rainbow is a sensing, living presence with feelings and thoughts, listening and speaking across the species barrier to human persons. Embedded in an environment filled with the signs and intentions of non-human persons, animistic people read the messages in the night sky, thunder, and rain in the same way modern people read books and facial expressions, an intermingling of self and world reflective of the in-between zone of soul and imagination described in chapter 3. As David Abram writes:

> The earthly world is felt as a vast, ever-unfolding Story in which we—along with the other animals, plants, and landforms—are all characters . . . a terrain filled with imagination.[10]

This profoundly relational and participatory ancestral world view was once nourished into adult maturity, building upon childhood sensitivity to the living presence and voices of nature rather than denying them as an illusion. And for hundreds of thousands of years this was how humans lived. The idea of nature as separate from human did not exist. We were in nature, and of nature. We were the sky, wind, and soil. The animals were kin, an animistic imagining that is still there in our Stone Age ancestral memory, yet intensely vulnerable to relatively recent culture shifts beginning with the advent of agriculture, 12,000 years ago, then speeding up during the Industrial Revolution, 300 years ago, and now racing full pelt into a techno-digital future.[11]

If each generation is 30 years, only 10 generations have passed in the 300 years since the Industrial Revolution and only 400 generations have passed in the 12,000 years since the Agricultural Revolution. When we compare that to the 17,000 generations that have passed since the rise of Homo Sapiens as a distinct species, we can begin to appreciate that these recent cultural changes have not been long enough for significant evolutionary adaptation, the evidence of which is modern children chatting with imaginary friends and teddy bears.

The Colonization of Imagination

The once-upon-a-time seamless network of animistic social relations disappeared with the Agricultural Revolution. Contrary to popular conception, nomadic hunter-gatherers had lived lives of relative ease, with the natural world as a kind of bountiful parent, openly sharing her abundance.[12] While the switch to farming is thought to have initially been a labour-saving development, subsequent population growth led to a considerably increased workload in comparison with the hunter-gatherer lifestyle: the soil had to be turned and tilled; the crops planted, tended, irrigated, and weeded; high fences and grain stores constructed to protect the harvest.[13]

While pre-agricultural societies had no conception of ownership, the drawing of a line around a piece of land and declaring it "mine" invented private property. The world was no longer whole but divided between those who did and did not deserve social relations. Certain plants, animals, and places lost their status as animate persons and became inanimate objects to be controlled and manipulated. Hierarchical societies and politics emerged to order the status of bosses, workers, and slaves. Armies appeared to protect the crops from neighbours who were now competitors for scarce resources.

The cultural changes of the Agricultural Revolution created a new kind of person. The fences in the fields were also psychological fences and an alienation crept into human life, as evolutionary psychologist Bruce Charlton writes:

It is learned objectivity that creates alienation—humans are no longer embedded in a world of social relations but become estranged, adrift in a world of indifferent things.[14]

The learned objectification of the Agricultural Revolution also applies to common assumptions towards imagination. In the same way that plants, animals, and slaves became objects, so too do theories of imagination conceive of imaginal characters as "inner objects" and mental "material"—images in memories, dreams, and fantasies being somehow personal property, owned by the person doing the imagining, such as when we speak of "my dream" and "my Inner Child". As the Jungian therapist Robert Bosnak writes:

I understand the certainty that all imagined presences are subsumed by our personhood [as] an embodiment of the 19th-century, power-grabbing, colonizing ego . . . as it takes possession of our mind, making us desire to rule and subject.[15]

To speak of a character of imagination as an "inner figure" or "subpersonality" carries a tinge of this colonialist thinking. In the same way that the European nations, viewing themselves as a superior race, set out to conquer and subdue the "savages" they encountered while exploring the globe, so also can identifying as the-person-doing-the-imagining turn waking dreams into an egocentric colonization project. This stance imposes our desires onto the native imagery of the psyche, assuming what is best rather than seeking to learn what we can by acknowledging a strange territory we do not understand, own, or control. To rush in to a waking dream in this way is not a lot different from how Christopher Columbus described his first impressions of the indigenous peoples he met:

They would make fine servants. . . . With 50 men we could subjugate them all and make them do whatever we want.[16]

While contemporary psychotherapy avoids imposing such a controlling agenda upon clients, many image-based techniques happily conceive of "using", "owning", "controlling" and "mastering" the figures met in imagination. The empathic respect towards the client at the heart of all relational therapies is a courtesy often not at all applied to imaginal characters. For example, in psychosynthesis, imaginal characters or subpersonalities are often taken as inferior images in need of refinement. As psychosynthesis therapist Piero Ferrucci writes:

> Subpersonalities . . . are degradations or distortions of timeless qualities existing in the higher levels of the psyche . . . the obstinate subpersonality may be seen as a distortion of will; and so on.[17]

Those subpersonalities deemed by the therapist to be distorted or inferior are worked upon to develop their potential. In this way, the subpersonality is not so much a living subject but a psychological object, a sub-part of the personality to be manipulated and changed.

Whether or not this approach deserves colonial comparisons, the important point for our purposes is that any quick move to utilize and manipulate imagery will undermine animistic imagination. Sometimes subpersonalities do develop and change, but to assume they all need to do so is to objectify them as a problem to be solved, not a person to be met and understood. To avoid this rush towards objectification we might ask, "Who is the judge of what is distorted?" and "Who is this development for?" Our answers will create a decentralized stance, a movement towards being just another image among images, rather than an identification as the-person-doing-the-imagining, an animistic participation with imaginal persons rather than a control over psychological objects.

The colonization of imagination is a collective cultural amnesia, one in which we have forgotten what we have forgotten, a loss of not just a theoretical understanding of animistic imagination but a whole way of being and acting in the world. The effect is not neutral. Theodore Roszak suggests the repression of animism by each generation requires "a wrenching effort, and a painful one to maintain . . . we call that pain, neurosis".[18] Roszak suggests that this individual suffering fuels the profound levels of alienation needed for industrial civilization to so plunder and pollute the natural world.[19]

David Abram similarly links the collective ecological with the personal psychological:

> To shut ourselves off from these other voices, to continue by our lifestyles to condemn these other sensibilities to the oblivion of extinction, is to rob our own senses of their integrity and to rob our minds of their coherence. We are human only in contact and conviviality with what is not human. Only in reciprocity with what is Other do we begin to heal ourselves.[20]

This healing takes the form of a recollection of what we once had, rather than the forging of an entirely new ability, and involves a recovery of a lost animistic imagination as an antidote to the alienation and objectification of modern life.

We will explore practical strategies for doing this in the following Waking Dream chapter, not as a pejoratively romantic or regressive return to childlike innocence but as a remembering and renewal in mature adult life of an imaginative ability at the heart of human potential.

1. Laura Sewall, *Sight and Sensibility: The Ecopsychology of Perception* (New York: Penguin Putnam, 1999), 122 (quoting Erazim Kohak).

2. James Hillman, *Re-Visioning Psychology* (New York: Harper Perennial, 1992), 39.

3. Graham Harvey, *Animism: Respecting the Living World, 2nd ed.* (London: Hurst, 2017).

4. Jay Griffiths, *Kith: The Riddle of the Childscape* (London: Penguin Press, 2013), 84.

5. David Abram, *The Spell of the Sensuous* (New York: Vintage Books, 1997), 131.

6. Theodore Roszak, *The Voice of the Earth: An Exploration of Ecopsychology* (Grand Rapids, MI: Phanes Press, 2001), 320.

7. Emma Restall Orr, *The Wakeful World. Animism, Mind and the Self in Nature* (New Alresford, UK: Moon Books/John Hunt Publishing, 2012).

8. David Abram, *Becoming Animal: An Earthly Cosmology* (New York: Penguin Random House, 2011), 268.

9. Richard K. Nelson, *Make Prayers to the Raven: A Koyukon View of the Northern Forest* (University of Chicago Press, 1983), 14.

10. David Abram, *Becoming Animal: An Earthly Cosmology* (New York: Penguin Random House, 2011), 270.

11. Paul Shepard, "Technology, Trauma, and the Wild," in *Ecopsychology: Restoring the Earth, Healing the Mind*, Ed. Theodore Roszak, Mary E. Gomes, and Allen D. Kanner (Berkeley, CA: Counterpoint Press, 1995), 21.

12. Marshall Sahlins, *Stone Age Economics* (Abbingdon, Oxon.: Routledge, 2017).

13. James C. Scott, *Against the Grain: A Deep History of the Earliest States* (New Haven, CT: Yale University Press, 2017).

14. https://www.hedweb.com/bgcharlton/animism.html

15. Robert Bosnak, *Embodiment: Creative Imagination in Medicine, Art and Travel* (Abbingdon, Oxon.: Routledge, 2007), 22.

16. Sarah Blaffer Hardy, *Mothers and Others: The Evolutionary Origins of Mutual Understanding* (Cambridge, MA: Harvard University Press, 2009), 27.

17. Piero Ferrucci, *What We May Be: Techniques for Psychological and Spiritual Growth through Psychosynthesis* (New York: Tarcher Putnam, 1982), 55.

18. Theodore Roszak, *The Voice of the Earth: An Exploration of Ecopsychology* (Grand Rapids, MI: Phanes Press, 2001), 304.

19. Ibid. 82.

20. David Abram, "The Ecology of Magic", in *Ecopsychology: Restoring the Earth, Healing the Mind*, Ed. Theodore Roszak, Mary E. Gomes, and Allen D. Kanner (Berkeley, CA: Counterpoint, 1995), 315.

Chapter 6

Waking Dreams No. 3 — Dialoguing

Only by affirming the animate-ness of perceived things
do we allow our words to emerge directly from the
depths of our ongoing reciprocity with the world.
—David Abram[1]

When it comes to psyche's speech . . . we listen so quickly
with our minds that we forget to hear. We don't give psyche's speech time to wander in the labyrinth of the ear.
—Russell Lockhart[2]

Psychotherapy is one of the few places where adults are actively
encouraged to engage in imaginal dialogues. In consulting rooms
across the land, conversations are going on right now between
human clients and non-human photographs, drawings, sculp-
tures, and maybe even the occasional teddy bear and potted plant.

Perhaps a client might be invited to imagine a character from
a recent dream as-if they were occupying an empty chair in the
corner of the room, an imaginal presence with a direct or avoidant
gaze, a smile or dark stare—a nonverbal communication that with
careful handling can turn into dialogue.

Dialoguing requires more than just a simple perception of images, hence the need for careful handling. To dialogue requires
granting images the personhood of animistic imagination, as described in the previous chapter. Inanimate objects don't talk; only
animate or living beings can communicate, as we find in nightly
dream conversations and the feral spontaneity of childhood play,
where princesses and frogs, books and broomsticks, rocks and
trees are all sentient creatures invested with the power of speech.
So too in a waking dream, there are no inanimate objects; all are
living subjects with whom we can enter into imaginal dialogue,
an invaluable means for the deepening of imaginative life.

In this third in the series of Waking Dream chapters, we draw upon the context of animistic imagination to present the principles and practices that allow conversation with imaginal characters. We begin with a breakdown of this imaginative terrain into three steps before going on to offer strategies, examples, and exercises for both "eyes-wide-open" and "eyes-closed" waking dream dialogues.

Dialoguing in a Waking Dream: The Three Steps

The implicit assumption in many therapy trainings and books is that imaginal dialogues in waking dreams are no different from everyday conversation. On a good day, this works by suggesting the convincing reality of an actual dream, in which communication does often proceed as it does in normal life. On not such a good day, this assumed equivalence between physical and imaginal conversations is not at all helpful. If the imaginal characters remain mute, and we have no other ideas how best to proceed, then the attempt at dialogue will be over before it has even started.

This leads to an impasse with two common outcomes: first, giving up and simply abandoning the possibilities of dialogue; second, making up something and unwittingly filling the silence with what we think the imaginal character might say. Self-invented speech can be an interesting reflective exercise, but it will be a dialogue within the boundaries of the habitual self, rather than a transformative non-egoic imaginal encounter.

While it is difficult to say for sure what is and is not self-invented speech, the accompanying feeling tone is a good indicator. Self-invented speech is marked by a forced feeling and a sense of calm confidence; genuine imaginal dialogues will feel much more spontaneous and usually have an edgy, out-of-control vulnerability created by an openness to imaginal others as autonomous persons rather than controlled psychological objects. The good news is that neither the silence of giving up or the self-invented speech of making up are a failure to imagine; both these outcomes are only apparent difficulties, an inevitable early stage in the deepening of imagination needed to support dialogue.

Dialogue in a waking dream requires a subtle shift of attention from physical sounds to auditory images. This is a perhaps obvious but nevertheless neglected point. The physical soundscape of everyday life is simply there, whether we like it or not: radios, televisions, shouts in the street, and so on—sounds that impinge upon us without any deliberate involvement on our part. Of course, a neighbourly chat or dialogue with a psychotherapist will require a certain effort, but the basic ability to hear and respond is somewhat taken for granted.

In a waking dream, the sounds we listen for are not physical but imagined. While not as obvious as simple physical sounds, these auditory images are nevertheless a recognizable everyday experience. What we are listening for is that subvocal imaginal speech that chatters away in the background of awareness; for example, when we argue with our conscience (*But I just couldn't tell her*), battle with a critical superego (*Ah, come on, give me a break!*), cajole a wounded pride (*You can do it next time*), or make supplication to a higher power (*Please God. . .*). Sometimes, particularly with more extroverted people, this imaginal speech is given physical expression, perhaps addressing a reflection in the mirror, confiding in a pet dog, or talking to a family gravestone. But whether expressed out loud or not, imaginal speech is always addressed towards equally imagined others as part of an ongoing dialogue.

The following three steps describe how to notice and build upon subvocal communications as a basis for imaginal dialogues in waking dream practice. As dialoguing is a subset of waking dream exploration, the steps will be familiar from chapter 4, as an emphasis upon the communication aspect already present in the exploring steps of Novelty, Possibility, Action.

Step 1: Novelty

The assumption in this first step is that subtle communications have been passing back and forth ever since our attention was arrested by the novel image. The novelty in this step is therefore a refinement of attention upon the novel image that allows us to notice this pre-existing communication. The colours, textures, shapes, moods, and movements of the novel image will be telling a story; for instance, is a character looking towards or away, gently smiling or laughing, stationary or gesticulating wildly? All these details and the time taken to dwell upon them will be the basis upon which we begin to hear the imaginal speech from which a dialogue will then develop.

Step 2: Possibility

The second step begins when we notice imaginal speech towards the novel image. If we attend closely, the possibilities of what is to be said, and how, will further emerge and clarify; for instance, we feel good about a smiling character and would like to make a friendly gesture, perhaps a raised hand and a smile first, followed by a quiet hello; we feel disgust towards a smelly, greasy-haired character and are unsure whether to scream "Get away from me!" or ask "Are you okay?" Once again, as in step 1, there is no rush; a slowed-down process of imagining will be one that best maintains the quality of the hypnagogic state.

Step 3: Activity

The third step puts the imagined possibilities into action. What we want to communicate is expressed towards the novel image. At first, this may be some kind of nonverbal communication: a smile or a wave of the hand; a moment of contact that can pave the way towards verbal expression. The opening of spoken dialogue is best done sensitively, without taking too much for granted: a simple "Hello, my name is . . ." or "Hi, can we talk?" The dialogue then proceeds by looping back and repeating the above three steps: noticing what the novel image communicates in response to what we have expressed; considering the possibilities for further dialogue; and then active expression.

Waking Dream Dialoguing in Everyday Life

Family portraits, holiday mementoes, and coffee mugs can sometimes feel like meaning-filled presences, animate objects that draw us into dialogue, even if only in the privacy of subvocal self-talk. The exercise that follows offers a simple two-part structure to better notice and cultivate these everyday opportunities for imaginal dialogue as an "eyes-wide-open" waking dream.

The first part is similar to the outdoors "eyes-wide-open" waking dream exercises in previous chapters (exercises 2.2 and 4.1), but this time, we pick an object to focus upon rather than a place. Any readily available object we can hold in our hands will suffice, although something with interesting textures, shapes, and colours will be best. The time spent on imaginal sensations in the first part of the exercise avoids the common mistake of rushing prematurely into verbal dialogue. Only once a basis of imaginal attention towards the object has been cultivated do we progress to the three steps of imaginal dialogue in the second part of the exercise: noticing novel communications, considering possibilities of response, and active expression.

Exercise 6.1: Dialoguing with an Object

PART 1

Take your time to study the object you have chosen.

Notice your assumptions about the object, and put them aside so that you are as open as possible to what you have before you, without preconceptions.

Take in the underlying materials, textures, shapes, weight, colours, light and shade, lumps and bumps, that make up your object.

Use all of your senses: what you see, and also what you sense through touch and smell. What sound if any does the object make when you move it around? I won't force you to taste it, but feel free to rub your finger against it and give it a lick.

Learn as much as you can about the object.

PART 2

Step 1: Novelty

Now imagine that as you are aware of the object, it too is aware, watching, listening, and wondering about you.

Imagine that as you are permeated with consciousness, intention, and purpose, so too is your object.

Take some time to tune in to this presence before you.

Notice what, if anything, the object is communicating to you. It might not be in words.

Let the breath help you stay focused.

Step 2: Possibility

Notice when any subvocal speech emerges? What and how might you want to communicate with the object? Take your time to consider these possibilities.

Step 3: Activity

When you are ready, express yourself towards the object in whatever way feels appropriate: verbally or nonverbally, in words or gestures, song or dance.

Now listen again to how the object responds and slowly dialogue back and forth as above.

When you are ready, thank the object in some way and bring the exercise to an end.

Waking Dream Dialoguing in Psychotherapy

The following transcript continues on from where we left off in the "exploring" chapter, with me as the therapist Th: and my client Daphne Cl: now some way into the waking dream. Daphne has turned around in her airplane seat to describe the air steward approaching down the aisle, a short 20-something man wearing a smart waistcoat and purple tie. Here I take the presence of the air steward as an opportunity to try out the three dialoguing steps. Once again, as in the previous transcript section, the anxiety from Daphne's everyday life is found within the waking dream imagery. However, in this section something new begins to emerge. The safety of the waking dream as an imaginative workshop allows Daphne to try out alternative ways of being. Her normally compliant personality takes the unusual step of not just acknowledging an angry feeling but also expressing it—something that would have been much harder in normal life.

> Th: Does he say anything?
>
> *[The dialogue began with step 1: inviting a description of what is already being communicated by the novel image.]*
>
> Cl: No, he's just looking at me.
>
> Th: And what do you take from his expression?
>
> Cl: He's got this air of expectancy.
>
> Th: How can you tell?
>
> Cl: He's looking right at me. His eyebrows are raised slightly.
>
> Th: And what is that expression telling you?
>
> Cl: He knows I'm not meant to be here, that there's been a mistake.
>
> Th: And what's that like for you now as you look up at him?

[The possibilities of step 2 begin here by gently enquiring after Daphne's private self-talk response to the nonverbal communication from the air host]

Cl: I'm not sure about him.

Th: You are not sure about him?

Cl: No. He's a bit fake, you know, like he's just acting a part.

Th: How do you feel about that?

Cl: A bit anxiety making, to be honest, and a bit frustrated. I mean, really!

Th: So, he is standing there, looking right at you with this kind of fakeness about him, which is a bit frustrating.

[The strength of feeling was clear, but instead of reflecting it back in isolation, which could have taken Daphne out of the hypnagogic state, I worked to weave it together with attention towards the imaginal scene]

Cl: Yeah, just standing there. What a prick!

Th: Is there anything you would like to say to him?

[Dialogue step 2 continued by considering the possibilities of verbal communication]

Cl: *[Pause, and then in a quiet voice]* I want to tell him to give me a break.

Th: Okay, can you ask him out loud now?

[Step 3: Active expression. An invitation to speak out loud helps strengthen the hypnagogic state.]

Cl: *[Pause]* Er, no.

Th: You can't say, Give me a break"?

[As active expression was not forthcoming, I returned to spend more time in step 2]

Cl: No.

Th: Something tricky about it?

Cl: I don't want to get in more trouble. I mean, he could fine me or something.

[*The vulnerability suggested the edgy unknown of genuine imaginal communication.*]

Th: Mmm . . . [*pause*]. I can see you don't want to get in trouble.

Cl: Okay, I'll give it a go. I think I can say it now. [*Pause*] "Look, can you just stop looking at me like that and give me a break, okay?"

[*The acknowledgement of the fears has reduced the hold they had on Daphne.*]

Th: What's happening now? How does he respond? Does he say anything back?

[*In looping back to step 1, I got a bit carried away and asked three questions all at once, which can be confusing to the client.*]

Cl: He's pouring me a coffee.

Th: What with?

[*Imaginal sense description maintains the hypnagogic state*]

Cl: One of those metallic flasks with a pouring spout, into a paper cup. The coffee is really hot. It's steaming.

Th: Does he not say anything?

[*Sticking with step 1, what is communicated by the novel image.*]

Cl: He says, "Of course" and as he hands it to me, "There you are."

Th: And what is the tone of his voice?

[*The communication is more than just the content of what is said.*]

Cl: Neutral, indifferent, like he doesn't care.

Th: And what's that like?

[I moved into step 2 again, enquiring after Daphne's nonverbal responses.]

Cl: It's annoying.

[Here, strength of feeling was getting stronger, and we continued the dialogue into step 3 again before looping back again to step 1.]

The air steward did not kick Daphne off the airplane after all; in fact, quite the opposite—he poured her a coffee despite her angry demands. The belief that this assertion would only make things worse was not realized, a realization that will in due course spill over into further empowerment in everyday life situations, as we shall see developing in subsequent Waking Dream chapters.

The Therapist Role and Language

The style of language adopted by a therapist will directly shape and influence the quality of a waking dream. This is not an entirely new point. In earlier Waking Dream chapters, imaginative experience has been distinguished from analytical thinking-about images. The therapist's role has therefore been one of avoiding and ignoring interpretations, as figuring out what the imagery means will quickly undermine the hypnagogic state, removing the waking dreamer from the felt immediacy of the imaginal environment.

Here, we build upon this point by considering not just what to avoid but two features of an animistic style of speaking a therapist needs to offer in the facilitation of waking dreams generally, and waking dream dialogues in particular.

The first and foremost feature of animistic speech is an attribution of personhood to all things. Recollect that only animate or living beings can communicate; inanimate objects don't talk. The facilitation of imaginal dialogue therefore requires we address all nouns (persons, places, things) as subjects not objects. As James Hillman writes:

> To give subjectivity and intentionality to a noun means more than moving into a special kind of language game; it means that we actually enter into another psychological dimension. The noun takes on consciousness; it becomes personified.[3]

The direct use of analytical terminology, such as, for example, the Child archetype, the Child subpersonality or Inner Child at best only alludes to a personified approach. These concepts are abstractions, a once-removed way of thinking-about imagery that fall short of embracing an animistic style of speaking. To speak of an Inner Child or Child subpersonality suggests that we are not really addressing an autonomous other but merely a symbol or representation of an inner configuration of feelings, thoughts, and behaviours—a psychological object not a living person.

In a waking dream all technical phrases are therefore eschewed in favour of a non-jargonistic everyday language, in which a child is simply a child never an Inner Child; an air steward is an air steward, never an "angry part of you"; and a dragon is a dragon, never an "internalized critic" or "superego", and so forth.

The second feature of an animistic style of speaking is a dynamic description of the whole. The emphasis is upon action and process rather than static objects and nouns. That is why the activities in the Waking Dream chapter titles and headings are expressed as gerunds (a verb form that functions as a noun)—entering, exploring, dialoguing, and so on. The waking dream is contextualized as an ongoing perception-feeling-thought-action narrative process. For example, rather than just a cigar, it is a man smoking a cigar, or even better a man smoking a cigar while writing a letter; and rather than just a child, it is a wide-eyed and tousle-haired toddler, playing with a doll and pretending not to have been seen. In this way, layers of connecting details create a joined-up sense of inhabiting an encompassing image environment. As David Abram writes:

> An animistic style of speaking . . . situates the human intellect back within the sensuous cosmos. It subverts the

long isolation of the thinking self from the perceptual world that it ponders, suggesting . . . that we are palpably entwined with all that we see, and hear, and touch.[4]

The analytical lexicon of psychotherapy is derived from modern European languages quite different from the speech of premodern animistic peoples. Modern languages emphasize the primacy of common nouns (a person, place, or thing) whereas animistic languages are verb-based.[5,6,7]

What modern languages describe as discrete things or persons are treated in animistic languages as dynamic events or processes, an emphasis that enhances the hypnagogic sense of involvement and belonging within the imaginal landscape. For example, "the wind" as a noun becomes the verb "it winds"; "the wind is hard" becomes "it winds hard"; and "I have a child" becomes "I live with child". While this translation into verb-based language is too clunky to use, and few will go to the trouble of learning an indigenous language, we can nevertheless take inspiration from animistic speech by remembering, as per the third entering step in chapter 2, to describe waking dreams as interconnected processes rather than a collection of fixed, stationary, and isolated things.

Exercise 6.2: Imaginal Dialogue and Writing

Writing is a form of dialogue. To put words down on a page or screen is less a solitary activity than a conversation with an imagined other. As many authors can attest, the writing process is not so much a hermetic act of self-invention as one of learning to notice and interact with the already existing presence of imaginal characters, actions, and speech in order to then write them down.[8,9]

This exercise, adapted from *Writing Your Way*,[10] is just one of many creative writing exercises that allow us to take advantage of this phenomenon without having to write a whole novel. It is a dialogue between dominant and non-dominant writing hands. All you need is a sheet of paper and a pen or pencil.

To start, place the pen in your dominant hand, the one you are accustomed to using, and open the dialogue by writing down a simple introduction or greeting (*Hello, my name is Allan*). Now continue writing with your other hand, the non-dominant hand, which offers a response to this opening (*Yeah?*). To which you respond with the dominant hand again (*Do you mind if we talk a bit?*) In this way, switching back between hands, a dialogue ensues.

What usually happens is that the unfamiliarity of writing with the nondominant hand interrupts the confidence and control of the habitual self, recreating the experience of when we first struggled to form letters on a page. This creates a vulnerability that can usher in a receptivity to imaginal voices and persons.

1. David Abram, *The Spell of the Sensuous* (New York: Vintage Books, 1997), 56.

2. Russell Lockhart, *Psyche Speaks: A Jungian Approach to Self and World* (Everett, WA: The Lockhart Press, 2014), 8.

3. James Hillman, *Re-Visioning Psychology* (New York: Harper Perennial, 1992),1.

4. David Abram, *Becoming Animal: An Earthly Cosmology* (New York: Penguin Random House, 2011), 70–71.

5. Russell Lockhart, *Psyche Speaks: A Jungian Approach to Self and World* (Everett, WA: The Lockhart Press, 2014), 32.

6. Murray Bookchin, *The Ecology of Freedom: The Emergence and Dissolution of Hierarchy* (Chico, CA: AK Press, 2005), p111.

7. *Rewild Yourself*, podcast, episode 12.

8. Mary Watkins, *Invisible Guests: The Development of Imaginal Dialogues* (Thompson, CT: Spring Publications, 2000), 93.

9. Iris Murdoch, *Existentialists and Mystics* (London: Penguin Press, 1999), 276.

10. Manjusvara, *Writing Your Way* (Cambridge, UK: Windhorse Publications, 2005), 73.

Chapter 7

Mechanical Imagination

Even the best attempts at explanation are only more or less successful translations into another metaphorical language.

—Carl Jung[1]

Metaphors matter because they give conceptual shape to life and we live within the dimensions of those shapes as if they were real.

—Jonathan Rowson[2]

The Newtonian view of the world as a mechanism operating in a fundamentally linear way came to Freud, as it did his contemporaries, indirectly, not so much from reading Newton . . . as through the ways that Newtonian ideals pervaded 19th-century science.

—Robert M. Galatzer-Levy[3]

Until this point, the critical discussion has focused on a theory of imagination related to the experiential ground of embodied, immersive, and animistic imagining. This chapter introduces a new line of enquiry into the role of metaphor in shaping the understanding of imagination. After a brief introduction to metaphor in general, and its close relationship to imagination in particular, this chapter will focus on the historical origins and continued popularity of the "mind-as-machine" metaphor in common approaches to imagining. What we will discover is that this mechanical metaphor reveals but also conceals significant aspects of imaginal experience, a nonmechanical imagining that is nevertheless treated as if it were a machine.

What is Metaphor?

The Latin word *metaphora* means to "transfer" or "carry over" experience from one domain to another. As one celebrated definition puts it, metaphor is a way of "understanding and experiencing one kind of thing in terms of another".[4] An everyday metaphor, such as "Life is a journey", is a way of carrying over the familiar and known experience of travel to communicate something of the nature of life. The known experience of a journey as a passage through time, with a beginning, middle, and end, during which we might learn a thing or two, is used to convey an understanding of the far more complex nature of life.

In this way metaphor helps us negotiate that which evades simple description and understanding by "as if" comparison with familiar and known phenomena. For example, life is "as if" it were a journey; time is "as if" it were money; and the male psychotherapist who reminds us of an early caregiver is "as if" he were a critical father.

Since Aristotle, metaphorical usage has been taken to be a merely poetical way of speaking; here, though, we shall be following the contemporary understanding of metaphor as primarily a form of perception that shapes all thinking, feeling, and sensation.[5,6,7] As James Hillman puts it, this is a broadly conceived understanding of metaphor as "a mode of being . . . a style of consciousness . . . a way of perceiving, feeling, and existing".[8]

To speak of life as a journey is not just a matter of speech. It communicates, for example, something of how we might feel about being halfway through the journey of life. Similarly, "Time is money" is not an objective statement of fact; it shapes the experience of time into a limited commodity, to be invested wisely and not squandered in idle dreaming. And even before anything is said about a psychotherapist being a critical father figure, the client's feeling, thinking, sensation, and action will be influenced by this metaphorical background.

In all these ways and more metaphor is more than just a way of speaking. In respect to our topic, we can say that metaphor is at the heart of how we imagine the world: "Every connection between things that the imagination "sees" or "draws" is a metaphor."[9]

Metaphor is imagining one thing "as if" it were another. To suggest that "Life is a journey" or "Time is money" is an act of imagination. Imagination is a process that draws upon known and familiar possibilities in memory and metaphorically transfers them into new and unfamiliar domains of experience—a transference, or carrying over, that is the same projective interplay of imagination described in preceding chapters as "the perception of images arising in between self and world".

In other words, the nature of imaginal perception is metaphorical. Whether reflecting on life as a journey, responding to a therapist as a critical father, or as we shall soon see, theorizing about imagination "as if" it were a machine, all imagining is imbued with metaphor. The enhancement of imaginative life can therefore be seen to go hand in hand with a parallel cultivation of metaphorical usage.

Freud and the Machine Metaphor

The metaphorical father of modern psychotherapy was Sigmund Freud. Major theoretical constructs in his thinking can be seen as a skilful combination of clinical observations with a rich tapestry of metaphors. Indeed, his writing is so laced with metaphor that an increasingly popular approach to the study of Freud is to consider him as a creative writer. This trend goes back to 1930, when he won the prestigious Goethe Award for writing in recognition of his contribution to literature. Freud himself did not present his work in psychology as fiction but as a bona fide scientific discipline; however, the Nobel Prize for Science, for which he was repeatedly nominated throughout his career, always eluded him.

In his novel psychological formulations Freud, influenced by the zeitgeist of his time, drew heavily upon technological metaphors. The transformational success of steam-engine thermodynamic technology during the Industrial Revolution had, as the historian Shamadasini writes, "far-reaching effects on social, psychological, and metaphysical thought in the latter half of the 19th century."[10]

The psychodynamic theory developed by Freud was a metaphorical carrying over of steam-engine thermodynamics into human psychology. In other words, the psyche hypothesized by Freud was imagined "as if" it were a steam-driven machine. Psychic energy was "as-if" it was compressed steam; only instead of water molecules this steam consisted of images, thoughts, and feelings. Psychic "objects" that interacted to create resistance, pressure, and force were imagined "as if" they were mechanical pistons and pumps, clashing away in the unconscious "as if" they were the hidden internal workings of a steam train; a mechanical metaphor that led to a psychoanalytical method that pictured a return of repressed unconscious material into consciousness "as-if" it were valves relieving excess pressure in a steam engine. As psychologist and educator Zachary Stein writes:

> Freud used several metaphors to describe the mind, but the one with the most exploratory power was the metaphor of the steam engine. "Psychic energy" was understood as if it were steam compressed within a chamber; bottle up too much energy and tension, and it will explode elsewhere as a neurotic symptom that you cannot understand.[11]

As a medical doctor, Freud was trained in the empirical method, designed to isolate the subjective bias of the scientist in order to better observe, predict, and control the objective world. As such, it was perhaps inevitable that his metaphorical framing paralleled that of empirical science; thus, just as scientists observed objects of the physical world, so too did Freud observe feelings, thoughts, and images as psychological objects within human subjectivity. The experimental procedures and explanatory methods of empiricism were metaphorically transferred into his psychoanalytic method. Often sitting out of sight from the patient and saying little, Freud conceived his role "as if" he were a neutral and uninvolved empirical observer. In this way, the mind-as-machine metaphor encompassed both therapist and client: the suffering client "as if" they were a mechanical breakdown; and the therapist "as if" they were a technician-mechanic.

More than a century after the introduction of Freud's concept of psychodynamics, the machine metaphor has become entirely woven into everyday language. In a technology-infused modern lifestyle, it intuitively makes sense to speak of ourselves "as if" we were machines like those all around us.

Freud's imagination reached out to steam engines and considered experiences "as-if" they were mechanical "stresses", "tensions", and "pressures"; today, it is digital machines that pervade everyday metaphors, when we speak of feeling "shut down", "stalled", "crashed", "fragmented", "switched off", and needing "a reset".

In all these ways and more, human self-experience is not just expressed but also experienced "as-if" it were mechanical, the result being a way of life focused upon an elusive emulation of mechanical predictability, order, and control. As psychotherapist Joseph Gold wryly puts it:

> Our great fear that computers and machines will come to run the world and displace us is less well founded than the more appropriate fear that we ourselves are unwittingly becoming more like those very machines.[12]

It is a therapeutic cliché that clients begin therapy imagining themselves as "broken" or "stuck" and wanting to recover a lost "efficiency" and sense of being "in control", a suffering that is assumed to be "as-if" a faulty component in need of repair or exchange for a better design. While this puts pressure on the psychotherapist to turn a switch and effect a sudden repair, most therapists would no more assist a client in these mechanistic fantasies than would a surgeon agree to amputate a healthy limb. Therapy works on a deeper level by addressing the fantasy of a mechanistic self, working to foster an acceptance and integration of the inevitable vulnerability and limitation that comes with human being, yet the mind-as-machine metaphor runs deep.

A Mechanical Theory of Imaginative Change

Despite not seeing themselves as therapist-technicians, many therapists do unwittingly apply image-based techniques that collude with a mechanistic theory of imaginative change. Popular visualizations, active imagination journeys, and role-plays assume images "as-if" they were mental "objects" or "parts" that can be adjusted to achieve predictable outcomes—a machine-based theory of change that can be recognized in the following three steps of mechanical reductionism, malfunction, and determinism.

Mechanical Reductionism

Mechanical reductionism is a process that simplifies complicated wholes into component parts, such as when a watch repair mechanic troubleshoots a stopped clock by dismantling it piece by piece to find the faulty component. Such reductionism is the first step in a mechanical theory of imaginative change. A single "part-image" will be separated from its context "as if" it were a mechanical component on a work bench.

Mechanical reductionism in many imaginal techniques can be seen in any treatment of an imaginal character or subpersonality that neglects the network of relationships that embed it within the encompassing imagery; for example, psychotherapist Piero Ferrucci writes: "Working on each of our subpersonalities, one by one, is the first, essential step."[13] In this way, the imaginal character is figuratively cut out and treated in isolation from the surrounding imagery and other characters.

The simplification of imaginal reductionism is also its limitation, as the child psychotherapist Donald Winnicott suggested, when he famously put it that, "There is no such thing as a baby." His point was not that babies are imaginary, but that it was impossible to understand a baby separately from the context in which it lives. A baby has no clear boundary separating it from its caregivers, environment, and cultural context. Considering a baby without reference to its wider context, as you would a discrete component such as a cog in a machine, is to impose an artificial boundary that does not exist.

As with babies, so too with images. Mechanical reductionism is a simplification that conceals the complexity of the whole, leading to a dangerous blindness not insight, as Zachary Stein writes can happen when:

> . . . truncated representations of complex phenomena are taken as sufficient and revelatory, when they are, in fact, insufficient and misleading. This is worse than flying blind; it is flying blind when you think you are seeing clearly.[14]

Applied to imagination, and mistaken for the whole truth, the mechanical metaphor of reductionism is a fantasy imagining of a machine that does not really exist. Imagination is only "as if" but not the same as a mechanical system.

Mechanical Malfunction

The second step of machine-based imaginative change is when one of the part-images is approached "as if" it were a faulty or defective mechanical component in need of repair—the assumption being that if only this malfunctioning imagery could be transformed into positive or healthy imagery, then psychological symptoms could be alleviated and transformed. As psychotherapist Piero Ferrucci continues with regard to imaginal characters or subpersonalities: "Subpersonalities . . . are degradations or distortions of timeless qualities existing in the higher levels of the psyche."[15]

Any strangeness of appearance or regressive behaviour in a subpersonality is taken as a distortion that needs to be developed. For example, a Vulnerable Child subpersonality needs to grow into adulthood; a Sexy Seducer subpersonality needs to be refined towards non erotic love; and a Stubborn subpersonality needs encouragement towards creative behaviours. In this way, so the thinking goes, we too will change along with the subpersonalities and become more adult, loving, and creative.

Once again, though, the machine metaphor is a simplification.

First, acceptable imagery is confined to the expected or normal. According to James Hillman, this is a "naturalistic fallacy" that misses the fact that events in imagination need not cohere to the standards of the natural world. As he puts it: "A multicoloured child, a woman with an erected penis, an oak tree bearing cherries, a snake becoming a cat who talks, are neither wrong, false, nor abnormal because they are unnatural."[16]

Second, to quickly label images as negative or faulty is a narrowing of meaning that often remains within the bounds of the egoic-personality. To assume that a Vulnerable Child, Sexy Seducer, or Stubborn subpersonality should be healed and made whole is to forsake the actual image presented, missing out on who we might become by relating to the imagery on its own terms rather than disciplining it into a desired self-image. As James Hillman writes:

> Disciplines of the imagination turn into a disciplining of the images. Insidiously, we become biased against the world we wish to enter. And active imagination becomes subverted into mind control, gaining knowledge, strength, and wisdom at the expense of the images of the soul.[17]

Hillman's "disciplines of imagination" are image-based techniques, so named because of a shared etymological root with "technology" in the Greek *technik*, which means "the rules, procedures, and skills used to achieve a particular end".[18] Whenever this particular end is fixing a faulty part-image, we are under the sway of the machine metaphor, a stance that pushes image-based approaches away from relating to "images of the soul" and towards creating a particular end result. In the same way that we do not need to understand how telephones, light bulbs, or cars work in order to benefit from their "particular end", so too does the assumption of imagination as a kind of machine neglect the process of how we imagine in a rush to create a predetermined content outcome.

Mechanical Determinism

The third step of machine-based imaginative change is mechanical determinism, the process by which a desired outcome is engineered by cause-and-effect interactions, as for example when a watch repair mechanic cleans, oils, or adjusts parts of the clockwork mechanism.

In the same way that a steam engine pulls a carriage along a railway track, so too is the inertia of a faulty part-image moved or changed by exposure to symbolic imagery chosen for its presumed transformative potential; typical examples being sunshine, a meeting with a wise being, or the ascent of a mountain. Hence the metaphorical notion of "powerful" and "strong" meditations and visualizations that "shift" and "overcome resistance". Piero Ferrucci writes of one such example, again with regard to subpersonalities:

> We can best facilitate this process [of developing a subpersonality] through purposeful imagery that deliberately uses the symbolism of ascent. The imagery of climbing a mountain represents, for example, the inner act of rising to the higher levels of our being.[19]

Ferrucci goes on to describe a waking dream in which we imagine walking with a subpersonality up a mountain path. As we ascend the mountain, it is suggested that we keep an eye on the subpersonality, who may undergo "subtle transformations—a variation in mood or facial expression or dress—or even radical transformation; that is, the subpersonality changing completely into something else".[19] Once at the top of the mountain, we are instructed to imagine sunshine pouring down, and again it is suggested that this may effect a further transformation that reveals "the very essence of your subpersonality".[19]

Ferrucci acknowledges that this technique may not result in any transformation of the subpersonality. The reason he offers is that unless a subpersonality is "recognized and accepted for what it is . . . we impede its journey".[19] However, to embrace the subpersonality for who they are as a strategy to immediately change them is at best a superficial level of acceptance, not to mention the nonacceptance of assuming the subpersonality as a psychological object rather than an animate imaginal subject or person, which, as we saw in chapters 5 and 6 is a requirement for any genuine non-egoic imaginative interaction.

While purposeful symbolic imagery and scenes are intended to offer a productive route to change, the adherence to this predetermined blueprint or formula is once again a mechanical simplification that neglects other possibilities inherent within the imagery. As Mary Watkins puts it:

> The possible beneficial results of having a person establish contact with his imagery and learn to move in that realm is compromised by a detailed schedule of places to get to and things to be accomplished . . . there is a harm, I believe, in not being willing to wait for the client to generate his own symbolic situations and modes of being. The therapist assumes a set way of being and teaches them . . . but this is not helping the patient to find his particular way. These two kinds of "therapy" should be differentiated.[20]

In the same way that a machine cannot change by itself but requires some form of external intervention, so too does a mechanical imagination require the person-doing-the-imagining and/or a therapist to intervene as an imaginer-technician, an approach that risks imposing a particular idea of change and misses out on the well-recognized creative and self-regenerative quality of imaginative experience. As Daniel N. Stern writes: "If the therapist thinks she knows [where the session is going], then she is treating a theory not a person."[21] The danger is that there is pressure to imagine-on-demand what is prescribed, resulting in a manufactured or made-up feeling, a push-button imagining that again emphasizes *the content* of what is imagined over the process of *how* we imagine.

Mechanical determinism fosters a fantasy of being able to design, engineer, and control imagination at will; however, simply learning to apply an imaginal technique will not necessarily result in the creation of whatever new feeling, insight, or behaviour we so desire. No matter how detailed and prescribed the technique, there will always be spontaneous imaginings along the way that deviate from the pre-planned formula.

In the above-described mountain technique, Ferrucci acknowledges the possibility that the subpersonality "may even degenerate", yet even an acceptably improved-upon subpersonality will also be an unplanned image. The mountain technique only specifies the means to achieve such a result (the ascent, the sunshine, and so on) not the exact nature of the crucial transformation or "particular end", which is neither predicted nor controlled.

In other words, these imaginal techniques are not entirely mechanical. If they were, then success would be guaranteed each and every time, like turning on a light switch. Clearly it is not that simple; the mechanical metaphor is not the whole story.

Living and Dead Metaphors

Freud's psychodynamic theory is still very much in use today. While a more relational and empathic stance towards the client has evolved, the basic premise of psychological objects and the forces between them remains a largely unaltered theoretical understanding across many orientations, as we have seen in regard to an inner imagination filled with images as mental "objects", or "parts". The mind-as-machine metaphor has stood the test of time. In part, the longevity of this metaphorical ground is due to the fact that it does indeed reveal something of the nature of imagination:

1 Images in memories and dreams do seem to be personal and subjective, "as if" they were contained within the workings of a mind as machine.

2 In any imaginal narrative certain images do stand-out "as if" they were discrete mechanical component parts.

3 Imaginal narratives often have a dramatic tension or conflict between these stand-out images "as if" they were oppositional mechanical forces.

4 Images can be altered by applying therapeutic techniques
and tools "as if" by mechanical manipulation.

We can imagine the *aha!* moment when Freud first pictured
imagination "as if" it were a complicated machine by recollecting
when we came across psychodynamic ideas for the first time. An
introduction to subpersonalities, inner objects, and the unconscious can seem revelatory, even magical. What before was a dim
mystery takes on a newfound structure and meaning.

The immediacy of this fresh metaphorical usage is what psychotherapist Terry Marks-Tarlow calls "living metaphor": a fluid
and malleable perception that exists at the boundary of self-experience as it comes into being.[22] It is seen most clearly during any
interruption to business-as-usual expectations. There is a living
and creative edge to metaphor as it reaches out into uncertainty,
exploring the gap between the familiar and strange, seeking out
the best-fit pictures and stories to help establish meaning. However, these benefits can obscure a down side to the explanatory
power of metaphor.

Metaphorical "as-if" comparisons are not exact. While metaphor reveals connective similarities, it also obscures and conceals
differences. For example, a popular metaphor among trainee therapists is "driving a car". The awkward opening stages of trying out
image-based approaches are understood "as if" they were the self-
consciously incompetent frustrations of learning to drive. The
metaphor anticipates that facilitating waking dreams will, with
practice, become a familiar, skilled, even somewhat automatic and
mechanical process, "as if" we are driving a car, which does reveal
something of what can happen. Skills and a semblance of compe-
tent familiarity will hopefully emerge over time. However, the
metaphorical comparison is only partial.

The metaphor also conceals that imagining is not a mechanical
process under the direct control of a therapist-as-driver, one in
which we simply turn the ignition to start, press the accelerator
to move forward, brake to slow down, and turn the steering wheel
in whatever direction we want to move next.

Imaginative process, as we have seen throughout the Waking Dream chapters, is often slow to begin, does not always speed up whenever we wish, and can take many unexpected twists and turns, all of which is concealed by the driving metaphor. Imagination is only "as if" but not the same as a machine. The metaphorical comparison is only partial, revealing something of imagination, as listed above, but also concealing other important aspects of imaginative experience:

1 Imaginal perception occurs between self and world, not just within a personal and subjective inner imagination.

2 Images are embedded in a network of relationships, not easily isolated into discrete, stand-out component parts.

3 Images interact, but not always according to Newton's mechanical law of equal and opposite forces.

4 Images are not always amenable to predictable change by therapeutic techniques.

Psychodynamic theory is metaphor, a way of imagining imagination "as if" it were the internal workings of a machine. However, with repeated usage and familiarity the imaginal background to the metaphor can become forgotten, the partial clarity offered being mistaken for a complete truth. The metaphorical reveal is over-emphasized, and the metaphor becomes the only way of seeing, rather than just one of many ways of seeing. What was a living metaphor becoming reified as a literal reality, what Marks-Tarlow calls a "dead metaphor": a habitual and fixed metaphorical usage that is unable to adapt to the immediacy of lived experience.[22] Here the overlap between metaphor and imagination becomes apparent once again, a dead metaphor being analogous to the fantasy imagining described in earlier chapters.

In conclusion, a mechanical imagination is "as if" it were the Wizard of Oz, a powerful idea that promises much but when we pull back the curtain appears as a little old man blowing into a microphone, at best an only partial understanding and approach to imagining.

The imagery presented in psychotherapeutic work, as we have seen, arises in spontaneous and unpredictable ways, proceeding indirectly by roundabout routes, taking unexpected and decidedly nonmechanical twists and turns; yet, experienced therapists, while perhaps cognizant of having little direct control over imagination—certainly not the capacity to fine-design it like an engineer—remain ill served by conventional psychodynamic theories rooted in the mind-as-machine metaphor. The result is an uneasy tension, with a nonmechanical imagining treated "as if" it were a machine, placing unrealistic pressure on therapists and clients alike to achieve steady deterministic progress.

Having established the limitations of a mechanical imagination, the book will now go on to explore alternative metaphors that better reveal the unpredictability of imaginative change and transformation.

1. Carl Jung, *The Archetypes and the Collective Unconscious* (Collected Works, Vol. 9, Part I), 160

2. Jonathan Rowson, *The Moves that Matter: A Chess Grandmaster on the Game of Life* (London: Bloomsbury Publishing, 2019), 27.

3. Robert M. Galatzer-Levy, *Nonlinear Psychoanalysis: Notes from Forty Years of Chaos and Complexity Theory* (Abbingdon, Oxon.: Routledge, 2017), 209.

4. George Lakoff and Mark Johnson, *Metaphors We Live By* (University of Chicago Press, 2003), 5.

5. Arnold H. Modell, *Imagination and the Meaningful Brain* (Cambridge, MA: MIT Press, 2003), 27.

6. George Lakoff and Mark Johnson, *Metaphors We Live By* (University of Chicago Press, 2003), 5.

7. Robert Romanyshyn, *Psychological Life: From Science to Metaphor* (Milton Keynes: The Open University Press, 1982).

8. James Hillman, *Re-Visioning Psychology* (New York: Harper Perennial, 1992), 56.

9. Peter Murphy, Michael A. Peters, et al, *Imagination: Three Models of Imagination in the Age of the Knowledge Economy* (Bern, Switzerland: Peter Lang Publishing, 2010), 2.

10. S. Shamadasani, *Jung and the Making of Modern Psychology: The Dream of a Science* (Cambridge University Press, 2003), 202.

11. http://www.zakstein.org/your-mind-is-not-a-computer-again-with-table/

12. Joseph Gold, *The Story Species: Our Life-Literature Connection* (Markham, Ontario, Canada: Fitzhenry and Whiteside, 2002), 167.

13. Piero Ferrucci, *What We May Be: Techniques for Psychological and Spiritual Growth through Psychosynthesis* (New York: Tarcher Putnam, 1982), 53.

14. Zachary Stein, *Education in a Time between Worlds: Essays on the Future of Schools, Technology, and Society* (San Francisco, CA: Bright Alliance, 2019), 147.

15. Piero Ferrucci, *What We May Be: Techniques for Psychological and Spiritual Growth through Psychosynthesis* (New York: Tarcher Putnam, 1982, 55.

16. James Hillman, *Re-Visioning Psychology* (New York: Harper Perennial, 1992), 84–85

17. Ibid, 39.

18. https://en.wikipedia.org/wiki/Techne

19. Piero Ferrucci, *What We May Be: Techniques for Psychological and Spiritual Growth through Psychosynthesis* (New York: Tarcher Putnam, 1982), 56–57.

20. Mary Watkins, *Waking Dreams* (Thompson, CT: Spring Publications, 2003), 60–61.

21. Daniel N. Stern, *The Present Moment in Psychotherapy and Everyday Life* (New York: W.W. Norton & Company, 2014), 156.

22. Terry Marks-Tarlow, *Psyche's Veil: Psychotherapy, Fractals and Complexity* (Abbingdon, Oxon.: Routledge, 2008), 109.

Chapter 8

Waking Dreams No. 4 — Shapeshifting

Let me sing to you now, about how people turn into other things.

—Ovid, Metamorphoses[1]

If we think the only way we can move in imaginal space is as we are in daily life, our ignorance and conscious preference limit our movement severely.

—Mary Watkins[2]

The closer we get to an image presence, the more it becomes an environment in which we find ourselves. We are pulled into the presence and participate in its medium . . . a movement outside of our selves, changing our state of being.

—Robert Bosnak[3]

It was as though I were no longer entirely located over here, where my body was sitting, for some piece of me had also gathered itself over there, beneath the purple sheen in the night-black feathers of the bird.

—David Abram[4]

This Waking Dream chapter departs from the established pattern of a practical application of the ideas presented in the preceding theoretical chapter. The Mechanical Imagination chapter was a largely polemical discussion of the limitations placed upon imaginative life by the mind-as-machine metaphor. Instead of providing further examples of a mechanistic imaginal, we now begin the presentation of a non-mechanical imagining, which will continue for the remainder of the book.

Perhaps appropriately, we start by exploring the decidedly non-mechanical phenomenon of imaginal identification: the empathic ability of living beings to enter imaginatively into the experience of another living being. The advantage of this is that it allows a movement beyond the boundaries and limiting biases of habitual self-identity, a transformative shift of viewpoint into the wonder of a baby, the stealth of a blackbird or the stillness of a tree. While a fulsome entry into another being is a perhaps fantastical notion, the stuff of ancient legends and science fiction, imaginal identification—or shapeshifting, as we shall be calling it—is a surprisingly common yet overlooked aspect of psychotherapy and everyday life.

Shapeshifting is most obviously at play whenever a good story takes us out of ourselves and we are transported into another life and world. It is an imaginative "absorption" that shifts the centre of imagining, or point of view, into the seeing, feeling, and thinking of a fictional character—as also seen in the ability of an actor to inhabit a character's physical shape and style of consciousness.

But we need not stop with the arts. Whenever we place our attention on something in a sustained way— a novel, movie, or painting; a person, place, or object—the centre of imagining is able to flow outwards, becoming decentred from the habitual self and taking up residence in a non-egoic perspective. Psychotherapists are trained to notice this fluidity of identity. It is cumbersomely called "countertransference", the slow shift in point of view that happens when, through careful attending to the client, the therapist comes to feel, think, and even sense in their body the feeling, thinking, and sensations of the client. Shapeshifting is at the empathic heart of not just therapy but all intimate relationships, as the psychoanalyst Daniel N. Stern writes:

> Our nervous systems are constructed to be captured by the nervous systems of others, so that we can experience others as if from within their skin, as well as from within our own. A sort of direct feeling route into the other person is potentially open, and we resonate with and participate in their experiences, and they in ours.[5]

Imagination makes porous beings of us all. Shapeshifting is not confined within but reaches outwards and intermingles with the lives of others. It is an innate imaginative ability that can be seen in many image-based therapies—active imagination, guided imagery, dramatherapy, family constellations, and the Gestalt "empty chair" method—all of which draw upon the healing possibilities of moving the centre of imagining into that of non-egoic figures. That said, the psychological literature of these therapies shows a remarkable lack of curiosity towards the "what" and "how" of shapeshifting, and the process of imagining is once again, as we have seen throughout the book, largely taken for granted; instead, these therapies focus on the insights and healing that can result from shapeshifting rather than attending to the conditions required to facilitate its occurrence.

My intention in this chapter is to present the neglected area of how to shapeshift by exploring the following practical questions: What are the principles of shapeshifting? How does it work? And what strategies and skills are needed to shapeshift in waking dreams?

Identity and Experience

Shapeshifting requires that we distinguish between identity and experience, a distinction we can most clearly make by recollecting that brief period in early life when we were all shapeshifters—a time when we spontaneously adopted the voices, actions, feelings, and thoughts of puppies and princesses, leprechauns and letterboxes, then back to normal again just in time for dinner; a time when the line between the literal and imaginal, real and unreal, was a blurred one.

As a personal example, one of my earliest memories is of crawling around a neighbour's lounge and proclaiming, "I'm not Allan; I'm a lion! *Grrrr!*" And in my child-like way, I really believed it; I was a lion. My sense of self was not yet consolidated, not yet firmed up, and I was able to play around with the act of identity and shapeshift into non-egoic characters.

Sooner or later, though, this malleable childhood ability begins to congeal and harden, and when adults start to tell children to "not be so silly" and to "grow up", a self-consciousness creeps in to shapeshifting. These subtle or overt judgements towards imagining effect a narrowing of shapeshifting ability, as children seek out the particular shape or identity that best allows them to rub along with the adult world. In time we hunker down around a stable identity—becoming "clever", "sensible", or "dutiful"—a particular spectrum of feeling, thought, and action that over long periods of time becomes just who we are, and we forget that it is really only one of many possible ways of being in the world.

Robert Bosnak writes of this forgetting as a conflation of identity with habitual consciousness:

> Identification with a particular singular sense of self is a learned habit, a conditioned reflex, creating our personal sense of subjectivity. . . . This, we learn from early on, is who we are. It is our habitual identification. We become so closely identified with it that we no longer know that the activity of identifying, and the habits of consciousness with which it is mixed, are two different elements.[6]

The cultivation of shapeshifting rests upon relearning the distinction between the two different elements of identity and experience. As mentioned above, therapists are trained to make this distinction. The idea of countertransference allows for the possibility that how a therapist feels and thinks will vary in accordance with the particular client they are sitting across the consulting room from.

At times these shifts in experience can be quite strong. I have often begun the day sitting with a client who left me feeling sleepy and depressed, fearful of having enough energy to continue with my sessions, only to find the next client evoking fantasies of being admired and a surfeit of enthusiasm for the work ahead. The trick, of course, is to learn to notice these shifts as they are happening. Even with a long therapeutic training, it can be all too easy to habitually identify with experience as personal rather than a contact with the client's experience; in other words, to realize that it is the *client* who is depressed or who is feeling admired and prized, not myself as the therapist. An appreciation of the possibility of shapeshifting is not enough; what is also needed is a practical understanding of how shapeshifting happens.

Shapeshifting in a Waking Dream: The Three Steps

The secret to shapeshifting is that it cannot be directly created. The amalgam of experiences that make up an identity are largely out of conscious control. All perceptions, from the smell of a rose to the sight of a shopping mall, evoke attendant feelings, thoughts, and sensations that arise spontaneously without any effort. To stub a toe, lose a job, or receive a legal notice will evoke pain, fear, anger, or whatever other response our particular identity deems fit. Of course, we can learn to notice these passing thoughts and feelings and have some influence over how we respond to them, but this does not stop them popping in and out of awareness like wild animals passing by in the night.

Just like approaching a wild animal in nature, shapeshifting cannot be approached directly. You can't stroll right up to it and expect it not to run away. As psychotherapists will readily testify, countertransference responses emerge slowly, as a result of spending time with a client. Similarly, novel readers will be familiar with the need to invest time in the first hundred pages or so of a book before feeling pulled into the orbit of the protagonist. This also occurs at the cinema, where absorption in a movie creeps up on us as a result of paying attention to the flickering screen images. In all these ways, we can see that shapeshifting is a gradual and indirect process.

A direct approach to shapeshifting is a fantasy of the mechanical imagination described in chapter 7, an assumption that experience can be manipulated and controlled by mechanistic techniques. If we try such a direct approach, we might assume a shapeshift has occurred, but most likely it will be a hypothetical reckoning from within the bounds of habitual identity; a thinking about what the other person might think, say, notice, and do, which is magnitudes of difference away from a genuine imaginal identification.

Yet this direct approach is the one promoted by many conventional image-based therapies, as might happen, for example, when a client in a waking dream encounters a dragon and the therapist suggests, "Now enter and become the dragon—look around with the eyes of the dragon, move as the dragon, feel as the dragon." In other words, identity is assumed to be an act of will, something that can be turned on and off like a lightbulb.

Admittedly, this does sometimes yield results. If the hold of habitual identity is sufficiently relaxed, a shift into another identity might happen—the waking dream continuing from the dragon point of view, soaring down mountainsides, and snorting flames at unsuspecting sheep. However, on not such a good day, this direct approach often fails. The hold of habitual identity is too strong to allow a shift into a new centre of imagining and the client remains locked into a familiar range of decidedly un-dragonlike feelings and thoughts, as Robert Bosnak writes:

> Identification is an involuntary, unconscious process and cannot be willed by the ego. By force of will I can empathize with another, imagine what another is feeling, put myself in someone else's shoes, but full identification is something that happens to me. Still, it is possible to create conditions under which identification is likely to occur.[7]

Shapeshifting is not controllable. If it were, the power of imagination could overcome insomnia, depression, or loneliness by simply entering at will into the mind state of a sleepy, happy, or in-love person. Sleepless nights, antidepressants, and dating websites would be a thing of the past, which is clearly ridiculous. All such issues are deeply woven into identity and seldom amenable to a sudden will-based transformation. However, there is something we can do.

In the examples given from fiction, child's play, and countertransference, the common conditions are an empathic attention over a period of time. That which we grant sustained attention and care towards will be what we are most likely to shapeshift into.

The following three steps are a breakdown of these imaginal conditions. While they offer no guarantee, they will make a shapeshift more likely to happen. As shapeshifting is a subset of waking-dream exploration, the steps follow the Novelty, Possibility, Activity template first described in chapter 4

Step 1: Novelty

This first step is a precursor to shapeshifting: a slow, steady, and sustained attention from the habitual identity towards the novel image we want to shapeshift into, including the feeling and thinking responses of this close study (as per the three "entering" steps in chapter 2). This happens, for example, when a psychotherapist carefully attends to the client's narrative, vocal style and tone, pauses, hesitations, facial expressions, movement, gestures, and so on, as well as their own feeling and thought responses. The effect is to stretch the boundaries of awareness outwards, creating the conditions for a movement of the centre of imagining.

Step 2: Possibility

Step two begins by allowing for the possibility that the feeling, thinking, and sensation we are experiencing as a result of the up-close attention towards the novel image in step 1 may be an out-of-character experience, signs that we are getting closer to the image presence of the novel image. This happens, for example, when a psychotherapist, after some time listening to a client, begins to notice a countertransference response; for example, the initially calm and confident feeling they had at the start of the session has now been replaced with an anxious anger.

Once the therapist notices an out-of-character response, they proceed in step 2 to focus upon it and allow it to emerge ever more fully. This happens alongside continuing to focus upon the sensory/feeling/thinking attention, as per step 1, but with one important difference: the shapeshifting process is now helped along by allowing the centre of imagining to become ambiguous; in other words, "the" feeling/thinking/sensation is attended to without attributing a pronoun location in either the habitual self ("my" feeling/thinking, and so forth.) or the novel image ("his" or "her" feeling/thinking, and so forth). In this way, a free-floating centre of imagining is created that avoids attempting to control the shapeshift.

Step 3: Activity

If shapeshifting happens, it will do so indirectly. By step 3, shapeshifting has taken place. Here, there are no instructions as such. Habitual identity, and with it all ideas about shapeshifting, has been left behind. We are now identified within the centre of imagining of the novel image—thinking, feeling, moving, and speaking as the novel image. All that remains is to explore the waking dream as the novel image, as happens when a psychotherapist falls unconscious to their countertransference and "acts out" by speaking from this new centre of imagining; for example, by talking impatiently to the client as a result of identification with an angry countertransference.

Waking Dream Shapeshifting in Everyday Life

Once again, the initial cultivation of waking dream skills in "eyes-wide-open" practice is a good place to start. In my local park, a friendly tree has taught me a lot about shapeshifting. On a windy day it is pleasant to shelter in the lee of its thick trunk, listening to the sway of branches, touching the bark, sinking my feet into the leaf mould, and smelling the soil. If I have the time to remain for a while, I notice that the manic rush of my habitual self is replaced with a rooted calm. Seconds and minutes seem to stretch out into seasons and years, and without even trying, I shapeshift into the perspective of the tree.

The instructions below apply to the above three steps as a loose framework for shapeshifting into any object that holds attention as a novel image, whether it be a familiar coffee mug or seemingly random but eye-catching found objects, such as feathers, leaves, and seaside shells.

Exercise 8.1: Shapeshifting with an Object

Step 1: Novelty

Take your time to notice the object with an attitude of interest and care.

Look to go beneath the labels of "mug" or "tree".

Be as open as possible to what you have before you.

Touch the object. Notice the surface texture and shape, the lumps and bumps, the rough and the smooth.

Notice how the light falls on the object.

What sounds, if any, come from the object?

What smells are there?

Move around the object. What else do you notice?

How do you feel in the presence of this object?

Savour the feeling for a while (even if you cannot put into words what you feel).

Notice the thoughts, sensations, movements, and gestures evoked in you.

Avoid getting into judgments or analyzing.

Use the rhythm of your breath to help you stay with your experience.

Step 2: Possibility

Notice any atypical or out-of-character responses to the object.

Notice hints that you are being drawn into the feeling, mood, and thought of the object.

Continue to refine your attention towards the object while also inviting these hints of shapeshifting ever further into awareness.

Continue to notice, and now allow the centre of imagining to become ambiguous, dropping the use of pronouns. For example, with a tree:

>Sense into **the** branches, not *my* sense of the branches or *its* branches

>Feel into **the** stillness, not *my* still feeling or *its* stillness

>Think with **the** slow calm, not *my* slow calm thoughts or *its* slow calm.

Step 3: Activity

Shapeshifting is happening or strongly emerging.

Go with the flow of imagining.

Sense, think, feel, and move as the object senses thinks, feels, and moves.

Waking Dream Shapeshifting in Psychotherapy

The following transcript continues on from where the earlier Dialoguing section left off, with me as the therapist Th: and my client Daphne Cl: now well into the waking dream.

In shapeshifting step 1, the pace of the waking dream, already slowed by dialogue, is reduced further still by inviting Daphne into a sustained up-close attention towards the air steward character with whom she has been dialoguing, an empathic observation that creates the pre-conditions for shapeshifting.

Step 2 begins when I recognize what might be some initial hints of shapeshifting and work to allow an ambiguity as to whether the centre of imagining is in Daphne or the air steward by dropping the usage of pronouns. The transcript ends with step 3—shapeshifting has occurred and Daphne explores the waking dream from this new air steward identification.

Th: What's happening now?

Cl: He's turned away sideways and is searching into his trolley.

Th: He's turned away from you. Okay. Can you tell me about his posture?

[step 1 begins with this first in a series of up-close attention enquiries.]

Cl: Yeah, he has these big shoulders, all hunched up. The hand near me is gripping the edge of the metal trolley.

Th: His hand is gripping the trolley?

Cl: Yeah, like really holding onto it hard and peering into it.

Th: And how far away is his face from you now?

[Maintaining the hypnagogic state by noticing the three-dimensionality of the imaginal environment.]

Cl: Not far. The trolley is almost touching my leg—less than a metre.

Th: Quite close then. And what is his facial expression?

[Concentrating on facial expression is a good route into the experience of the air steward.]

Cl: He's frowning. His eyes are cold and serious, like he's pissed off or something. I can hear him mumbling under his breath.

Th: Can you hear what he is saying?

Cl: Not really. [*Pause.*] No.

Th: Okay, but what's the tone of it? The mood of what he is mumbling?

Cl: Angry, an angry muttering, like he's irritated about something.

Th: Can you focus on that tone and his anger?

> [*Concentrating on the tone of voice further pulls the client into the experience of the air steward, which I was hoping would lead into step 2.*]

Cl: [*Pause.*]

Th: Can you slow it down and stay with his muttering? Is that okay?

> [*The pause suggested some kind of struggle. Here, my asking for permission conveyed an empathic understanding that this might not be easy.*]

Cl: Yeah. It feels like he's fed up with this job, being a waiter in the sky. It's stupid.

Th: He feels fed up.

Cl: And angry, not wanting to be here at all.

Th: Can you stay with that feeling for a moment...be with that angry, fed-up, it's-a-stupid-job feeling and thought.

> [*Daphne's last two feeling responses have sponta-neously shown an ambiguous centre of imagining: "It's stupid" and "angry", rather than "He thinks it's stupid" and "He is angry", so we are well into step 2 by now, and I simply continued this ambiguity as to the centre of imagining.*]

Cl: Yeah, it's really shitty. Frustration and some upset, too; a mixture of angry/sad.

Th: Can you feel that in *the* body?

[*Dropping the use of pronouns (avoiding your body and his body) to better allow for the possibility of a shapeshift.*]

Cl: I can't quite describe it.

Th: Just focus on *the* feeling. Don't worry about getting the right word. Breathe into the "felt sense" of it.

Cl: I feel it in the throat, a big lump, a stifled roar, and an upset cry together.

[*This is a long way from the fearful anxiety of Daphne's habitual identity*]

Th: A roar and a cry together.

Cl: Ah, my gosh! For f***'s sake! Come on!

Th: Come on!

Cl: [*Pause.*]

[*The centre of imagining seemed to be on the move, and I allowed a long pause to let Daphne dwell in this new point of view*]

Th: What is happening now?

[*Tentatively moving into step 3, wondering if a shapeshift has occurred.*]

Cl: I've had enough.

Th: And what is happening?

[*Wanting to embed the strength of feeling within the imaginal scene so as to maintain the hypnagogic state.*]

Cl: I'm pushing the trolley down the aisle. I'm done.

Th: What do you see?

[*The waking dream continued by addressing the thinking-feeling-perception-action of this new air steward identity directly, rather than saying "What do you see as the air steward?"*]

The Therapist Role and Point of View

An important consideration with regard to shapeshifting is what point of view the therapist's interventions are addressed towards. As we have seen, the client will move across three points of view during the shapeshifting process: in step 1, that of the habitual identity; in step 2, an ambiguous point of view in-between the habitual identity and the novel image; in step 3, finally arriving in the point of view of the novel image.

In order to follow the client through these steps, the therapist needs to judge when to switch point of views so as to avoid acting against the shapeshifting process. This is particularly important in "eyes-wide-open" waking dreams, in which the client's point of view can move, despite everyday appearance remaining more or less the same.

The following example of shapeshifting in the popular Gestalt "empty chair" method is presented as a means of considering an adjustment of point of view that will be applicable to other "eyes-wide-open" approaches, such as family constellations, psychodrama, and art therapy. The "empty chair" method invites a client to perceive and relate to an imaginal character (such as a dream figure, historical caregiver, or subpersonality) by imagining them sitting in the consulting room on an "empty chair" pulled out for this purpose.

A typical beginning would be for a therapist to suggest: "We've been talking about the dream witch for a while now, and it feels as if she is kind of with us in the room, so how about we acknowledge that by giving her a place on this chair?" The client will then be invited to describe the character, moving the session into the experiential immediacy of an "eyes-wide-open" waking dream. Often this initial description is followed by a dialogue, but here we explore the three steps of shapeshifting that occur in the other common development of the method, when the client is invited to switch chairs and identify with the imagined character.

Step 1: Novelty

In step 1, it is straightforward to recognize the client's description of the character on the empty chair as originating from the point of view of the habitual identity. The therapeutic task here concerns the direction of this point of view. In order to build up the hypnagogic state and imagine the character to be in the consulting room, it is important for the client to switch their gaze from the therapist towards the "empty chair". This is most simply done by the therapist themselves looking towards the "empty chair", which usually has the effect of the client following suit. If this does not work, a direct invitation to do so can be made. The hypnagogic state is then established by asking: "Can you tell me how you see the witch on the chair?" "How long is her hair?" "What is her facial expression?" "Is she looking at you directly, or not?", and so on.

Step 2: Possibility

A conventional approach to "empty chair" work often skips past step 2, with the therapist initiating shapeshifting with a simple invitation to switch chairs and "become the witch". However, as we have seen, direct attempts at shapeshifting will likely only result in a self-invented fantasy imagining: the thinking and feeling of a generic witch rather than a genuine identification with the surprising and quirky point of view of this particular witch character.

It is therefore important to avoid using the switching of chairs as a means to create a shapeshifting process—only once the shapeshifting process is strongly emerging will the therapist introduce the chair switch; hence, the importance of step 2 in continuing the up-close attention towards the imaginal character while looking out for any out-of-character feeling/thought/ perception responses that suggest a shapeshift is emerging.

At that point, the therapist will cease addressing interventions towards the habitual point of view, as to do so would only act against the possibility of shapeshifting by further anchoring the client within habitual identity; instead, interventions will be addressed towards an ambiguous point of view, for example: "Stay with *the* grumpy feeling", rather than "Can you focus upon *her* grumpy feeling?"; "Can you tune in to *that* irritation?", rather than "Can you notice *your* irritation?", and so on.

Step 3: Activity

Once the shapeshifting process is strongly emerging, the therapist invites the client to move into and sit in the empty chair. The important consideration in the chair switch is to refrain from any direct or explicit announcement of the shapeshift, such as often happens in a conventional approach; for example, when a therapist suggests: "Now move over and sit in the witch's chair. Take your time, and feel your way into being the witch. See as she sees. Move as she moves."

Any such explicit announcement of the shapeshift will once again undermine the process by re-anchoring the client in their habitual identity; instead, the chair switch needs to be an inadvertent rather than a self-conscious move—an elaboration of a shapeshift that has already happened, rather than an attempt to initiate it. What the therapist does not do is then clear enough. What is done is to simply address the invitation to switch chairs to the client's new "you" point of view; for example, "Can *you* come and sit over here?" "Tell me how *you* are feeling now?", "What are *you* noticing?", and so on.

1. Richard Powers, *The Overstory* (New York: Norton, 2019), 147 (quote).

2. Mary Watkins, *Waking Dreams* (Thompson, CT: Spring Publications, 2003), 113.

3. Robert Bosnak, *Embodiment: Creative Imagination in Medicine, Art and Travel*, (Abbingdon, Oxon.: Routledge, 2007), 20.

4. David Abram, *Becoming Animal: An Earthly Cosmology* (New York: Penguin Random House, 2011), 245.

5. Daniel N. Stern, *The Present Moment in Psychotherapy and Everyday Life* (New York: W.W. Norton & Company, 2014), 76.

6. Robert Bosnak, *Embodiment: Creative Imagination in Medicine, Art and Travel*, (Abbingdon, Oxon.: Routledge, 2007), 126.

7. Robert Bosnak, *Tracks in the Wilderness of Dreaming: Exploring Interior Landscape Through Practical Dreamwork* (New York: Dell Publishing, 1996), 31.

Chapter 9

Ecological Imagination

To the eyes of a man of Imagination, Nature is Imagination itself.

—William Blake[1]

Through active exercise of ecological imagination we are already healing ourselves and our environments.

—Steven Fesmire[2]

The major problems in the world stem from the difference in the way nature works and the way people think.

—Gregory Bateson[3]

A repeating theme across these theoretical chapters has been the interconnectedness of imagination. As I have shown, to imagine is to engage an amalgam of the senses, a co-creation of not just the seen but also the heard, touched, smelt, and tasted. Imagination forms an embodied perceptual relationship between self and world and a synthesis of the psychological functions operating within and through sensations, feelings, thoughts, intuitions, and actions; a fluid and shifting imaginal nature that we have seen to be ill served by those conventional therapeutic theories based upon a mind-as-machine metaphor.

In the search for a theory that reflects a joined-up, interconnected imaginal experience, this chapter sketches out the idea of an ecological imagination; therefore, instead of picturing imagination "as if" it were a machine, we shall be drawing upon metaphors from ecology and exploring the imaginal "as if" it were a living organism, a web or field of relations and energy flows.

For this, we shall be drawing upon recent work integrating psychotherapy with complexity theory, a contemporary scientific understanding of change that has emerged from the modelling of ecological phenomenon such as cloud formations, lightning pathways, and the beatings of the human heart. What we shall discover is a metaphorical ground for imaginal change much more closely aligned to the wildness and spontaneity of human imagining than the deterministic assumptions of a mechanical imagination, an alignment that provides a theoretical framework for working with those recognizable but perhaps overlooked aspects of both psychotherapeutic and everyday imaginal experience: the irregular, unexpected, and seemingly chaotic imaginings that, as we shall see, are those which most often point the way to creative process, healing, and transformation.

Images as Ecosystems

An ecosystem is the complex network of relationships that exists among plants, animals, and their environment. All the various forms of life in an ecosystem—bacteria, fungi, plants, trees, bugs, birds, and mammals—are in a continual state of interaction with each other and the surrounding soil, rocks, water, air, and sunshine. Each life form has a particular ecological niche that is dependent on other life forms and environmental factors.

Tiny bacterial organisms, for example, find a niche within the digestive tract of a host animal, which in turn finds a niche in a particular landscape and weather pattern, where it eats plants and falls prey to larger animals, and so on. Everything is connected. Matter, energy, and information flow across porous boundaries to the extent that it is difficult to say where one life form ends and another begins. An ecosystem is therefore studied and understood not as a collection of discrete actors or things but as a network of relationships. As ecopsychologist David Key describes with regard to a wave in a river,

> You can see the wave, you can photograph it, you can draw or paint it, you can point to it and other people will see it. . . . But if you scoop it out of the river in a bucket, it will vanish—only to be replaced by "another" wave. The

wave is created in a form that we experience as a "wave" by the rocks on the river bed, by the friction of air on the surface of the water, by any material moving through the water, by the dimensions of space the water has in which to flow, by the interactions of light and energy. The wave is a product of its environment. It is the result of an infinite amount of different relationships with everything around and inside it. When it is removed from these relationships, it vanishes.[4]

The wave can be seen, photographed, and painted. Its freshness can be felt in the air and touched by the back of a hand. We can even jump into the river and swim into and through the wave, but as soon as we try to separate the wave from its relationship to the surrounding ecosystem it vanishes and all we are left with is a puddle at the bottom of a bucket. Of course, nobody would try to scoop a wave out of a river. The idea is ridiculous, and yet, this is effectively what happens when conventional approaches to imagining assume that single part-images can be removed from the surrounding imaginal context or environment and treated in isolation.

To avoid images disappearing into the bottom of analytical buckets, as we have seen happens when interpretative thinking eclipses imagining, this book has already sketched out a theoretical and experiential approach that has implicitly described an ecological imagining, one that directs attention to participation within a process of imagining rather than standing back and analyzing it as if it were some kind of machine.

The embodied, immersive, and animistic aspects of imagination presented in chapters 1, 3, and 5 all drew upon ecological metaphor to reveal the interconnectedness of imaginative experience. Embodied imagination emphasized the synthesis of imagining "as if" it were the sensed sights and sounds, feelings, and thoughts of the human psycho-biological organism. Immersive imagination recognized that to imagine is to find ourselves "as if" we were in an encompassing imaginal environment, whether the purely imagined scenery of an "eyes-closed" waking dream or the streets, trees, and lampposts of everyday life as an ongoing "eyes-wide-open" waking dream. Animistic imagination spoke to the phenomenon of images "as if" they were living subjects, in the same way that people, plants, and animals are autonomous life forms. As Robert Bosnak notes:

> Images behave as ecosystems. Each element in an image-place is predicated upon the other, much like in a natural physical environment.[5]

Images exist within an imaginal ecology "as if" they were waves in a river. To imagine is to enter into and participate within this image environment "as if" we were walking along a river bank, an imaginal participation that we now consider through a brief introduction to complexity theory and its understanding of how change happens in ecosystems.

Fairy Tale Complexity Theory

Complexity theory is perhaps best known in popular culture as "the butterfly effect". This phrase originated in a question posed in 1966 by Edward Lorenz, the originator of complexity theory, when he asked, "Does the flap of a butterfly's wings in Brazil set off a tornado in Texas?"[6]

His question seemed bizarre. It flew in the face of conventional mechanistic theories that assumed large forces were needed to create significant changes. It was also an unanswerable question—there was no real possibility of measuring the effects of a particular wing flap from a singular butterfly.

Nevertheless, Lorenz posed his rhetorical question because he had demonstrated a generally recognizable "butterfly effect", or as he called it, "a sensitivity to initial conditions", in which small changes in what are called "complex systems" can, through multiple feedback loops, lead to large-scale consequences. The results of his breakthrough have since transformed the understanding of change in contemporary science.

While the question of tornadoes points to the origins of complexity theory in weather prediction, it was soon recognized to be a useful way of studying anything that was seen to function as an ecosystem. This includes traffic flows, communications technology, and business organizations, a list of applications that we now extend by introducing complexity theory in regard to image-centric therapy, following recent work by Terry Marks-Tarlow, Robert M. Galatzer-Levy, and others integrating it with psychotherapy more broadly.

Complexity theory offers three particular advantages for a theory of imaginal change that build upon the process-oriented imagining already sketched out in these pages. In order to relate these advantages, the basic principles of complexity theory—complex systems, the edge of chaos, and emergence—are now presented not in an abstract mathematical fashion but in respect to the famous Brothers Grimm fairy tale "The Frog Prince".[7]

Complex Systems

A complex system is best understood as an open system in which all the many parts are in a state of continual interaction with the surrounding environment. The open and porous boundaries of ecosystems, across which matter, energy, and information flow mean they are complex systems; for example, a tree is a complex system with leaves and roots that interact with the light, gases, humidity, and nutrients in the atmosphere and soil, which in turn are shaped by multiple interconnecting feedback loops within the wider ecosystem: human pollution, droughts and storms, animal and plant life, and so on. To understand how the tree grows and develops therefore requires a consideration of the whole complex system, and as with trees so too with images.

The idea of an ecological imagination, as mentioned above, reflects the interconnectedness of imaginative experience as a complex system with open boundaries. This is in contrast to the mechanical imagination presented in chapter 7. While an ecosystem is a complex system, a machine is called a "complicated system", the many intricate parts of which are contained within a boundary that separates it from the surrounding environment. A complicated system is therefore a closed rather than an open system.

A waking dream or any other imaginal experience—reading a novel, watching a movie, dialoguing with an "empty chair" in a therapy session—becomes a complicated system when analyzed into constituent sub-parts: Inner Children and subpersonalities, themes and characters from childhood history, symbols or representations of feeling states, and so on. This also happens when a fairy tale is taken as a kind of literary machine built from words, sentences, and paragraph parts; a text that can be separated into various themes, settings, characters, genre, and so on, the reading of which will lead to a predictable set of feeling and emotions:

> *Near the royal castle there was a great dark wood and when the day was hot, the King's daughter used to go forth into the wood and sit by the brink of a cool well, and if the time seemed long, she would take out a golden ball, and throw it up and catch it again, and this was her favourite pastime.*
>
> *Now it happened one day that the golden ball, instead of falling back into the maiden's little hand which had sent it aloft, dropped to the ground near the edge of the well and rolled in.*
>
> *The king's daughter followed it with her eyes as it sank, but the well was so deep that the bottom could not be seen.*
>
> *Then she began to weep as if she could never be comforted. And in the midst of her weeping she heard a voice saying to her, "What ails thee, king's daughter? Thy tears would melt a heart of stone." And when she looked to see where the voice came from, there was nothing but a frog stretching his thick ugly head out of the water.*

The classic text by Freudian psychoanalyst Bruno Bettelheim, *The Uses of Enchantment*, does a good job of breaking down this Frog Prince story into its underlying themes: the golden ball stands for the undeveloped narcissistic psyche, the loss of which is a loss of naivete; the frog character presages the discovery of sexual relations—as Bettelheim suggests: "It is difficult to imagine a better way to convey to the child that he need not be afraid of the (to him) repugnant aspects of sex than the way it is done in this story."[8] (This last point is a good example of how Freudian analysis frequently manages to make everything about sex.) However, the important point to make here is that these interpretations place us at a cognitive distance from the story. They do not immerse us within the story world but separate us from the content of what is imagined "as if" we were an engineer lifting the cover of a machine.

The first advantage of complexity theory is an understanding of the inseparability of imaginer from the process of imagining; for example, the Frog Prince story becomes a complex system when we consider it not as an isolated text, enclosed within the covers of a book to be analyzed by Freudians, but as an open system imagined through an interaction with a reader. In participation with a reader, the forest and pond, princess and frog come alive as an ecology of imagining:

> "I weep because my golden ball has fallen into the well."
>
> "Never mind, do not weep," answered the frog; "I can help you; but what will you give me if I fetch up your ball again?"
>
> "Whatever you like, dear frog," said she; "any of my clothes, my pearls and jewels, or even the golden crown that I wear."
>
> "Thy clothes, thy pearls and jewels, and thy golden crown are not for me," answered the frog; "but if thou wouldst love me, and have me for thy companion and play-fellow, and let me sit by thee at table, and eat from thy plate, and drink from thy cup, and sleep in thy little bed, if thou wouldst promise all this, then would I dive below the water and fetch thee thy golden ball again."
>
> "Oh yes," she answered; "I will promise it all, whatever you want, if you will only get me my ball again."
>
> But she thought to herself, "What nonsense he talks! as if he could do anything but sit in the water and croak with the other frogs, or could possibly be any one's companion."
>
> But the frog, as soon as he heard her promise, drew his head under the water and after a while he came to the sur-

face again with the ball in his mouth, and he threw it on the grass.

The King's daughter was overjoyed to see her pretty play-thing again, and she caught it up and ran off with it.

"Stop, stop!" cried the frog; "take me up too; I cannot run as fast as you!"

But it was of no use, for she would not listen to him, but made haste home, and very soon forgot all about the poor frog.

To read the fairy tale in a participatory rather than analytical fashion is to enter into the events of the story, as indeed, will spontaneously happen. Children and very few adults will find themselves thinking about narcissism and the repugnance of sexual relations, as they read the story; instead, immersive imagining will naturally draw them into the ecology of the fairy tale and its banqueting halls and bed chambers, an eco-imagining not limited to the actual text but a co-creation between reader and page that embellishes the written outline. A fairy tale or any other imaginal experience—viewing a painting, reading a poem, or exploring a waking dream—becomes a complex system whenever this interconnected participatory relationship is emphasized.

The Edge of Chaos

A complicated system is basically a machine that performs a specific task and keeps on doing that one thing until it breaks down. Whether a food mixer or a jet engine, complicated systems will never change, because they are designed to operate across a narrow range of operating conditions called a "fixed equilibrium".

Inside every machine is a regulatory control mechanism that maintains it within a precise operational range, a simple example being a central heating thermostat. If we want to change a complicated system, some kind of external intervention is required—someone turns the thermostat up or down, a chef changes a food mixer blade, or an engineer downloads new software into a jet engine.

If we take the Frog Prince story as a complicated system, change would require a writer to rearrange and add new words, hence the mechanical imagination assumption, discussed in chapter 7, of applying therapeutic techniques to engineer imaginal change. The disadvantage of this is that it is a manipulation that once again separates the imaginer from the process of imagining.

The second advantage of complexity theory as a basis for understanding imaginal change is that unlike machines complex systems do indeed change. Complex systems are able to change because they exist in what is called a state of "dynamic equilibrium" that allows a flexibility to respond to changing conditions. For example, a healthy human heart has a range of heartbeats across which it can operate. When we climb some steps it goes up, and when we fall asleep it goes down.

If we take the Frog Prince story as an example of a complex system, we can see this "dynamic equilibrium" in the range of possibilities the princess explores in response to the unwelcome and repeated reappearance of the frog.

To begin with the princess is happily sitting by the pond, playing with her golden ball. As discussed in chapter 2, this opening to the story is the kind of entry-point scene we want in order to begin a waking dream: a safe place that does not provoke challenging feelings or thoughts.

The princess's contentment while playing with her golden ball is not a mechanical "fixed equilibrium", for the appearance of the frog, which we can see as a novel image, interrupts the serenity of the entry-point scene, ushering in a dramatic tension to the story. This is a tension that complexity theory calls "the edge of chaos", a transitional zone with a mixture of flexibility and stability in which the creative possibilities for change are maximal. As Galatzer-Levy writes in relation to psychotherapy:

> Psychoanalysis may be seen as a method for freeing people from fixed patterns of thought, feeling, and behaviour and allowing them to creatively learn from experience. Doing this requires a degree of disorganization sufficient

to allow the exploration of novel possibilities, while at the same time maintaining sufficient organization so as to avoid the dual dangers of chaos or the precipitation of emergency rigid defences against it. Such a state is called the edge of chaos.[9]

The dramatic tension of the Frog Prince fairy tale can be seen as one that takes the princess into the possibilities offered by the edge of chaos. She does not continue daydreaming as a machine princess would, stuck upon a "fixed equilibrium", only able to do one thing over and over; instead, she employs successively elaborate strategies of feeling, thought, and action to get away from the frog.

> *The next day, when the King's daughter was sitting at table with the King and all the court, and eating from her golden plate, there came something pitter patter up the marble stairs, and then there came a knocking at the door, and a voice crying "Youngest King's daughter, let me in."*
>
> *And she got up and ran to see who it could be, but when she opened the door, there was the frog sitting outside. Then she shut the door hastily and went back to her seat, feeling very uneasy.*
>
> *The King noticed how quickly her heart was beating, and said, "My child, what are you afraid of? Is there a giant standing at the door ready to carry you away?"*
>
> *"Oh no," answered she, "no giant, but a horrid frog."*
>
> *"And what does the frog want?" asked the King.*
>
> *Once the princess had explained they all heard knocking a second time and crying, "Youngest King's daughter, Open to me!"*
>
> *"That which thou hast promised must thou perform," said the King, "so go now and let him in."*
>
> *So she went and opened the door, and the frog hopped in, following at her heels, till she reached her chair.*
>
> *Then he cried, "Lift me up to sit by you." But she delayed*

doing so until the King ordered her. When once the frog was on the chair, he wanted to get on the table, and there he sat and said,

"Now push your golden plate a little nearer, so that we may eat together."

And so she did, but everybody might see how unwilling she was, and the frog feasted heartily, but every morsel seemed to stick in her throat.

The frog's persistence escalates the dramatic tension, taking the princess further away from the stability of the entry-point scene into ever more novel and out-of-character situations. The relational dynamic between the princess and frog—as between parent and child, therapist and client—has created a combined complex system with an increased range of possibilities that the princess would not have had without the frog. As the princess is nudged into an ever more fulsome participation with the loathsome frog, we reach the point in the story of maximal disorganization beyond which the dramatic tension would collapse into complete chaos or defensive avoidance. As Robert Bosnak describes:

Complexity theory posits that on the border between order and chaos—on the verge of going out of control, but not entirely . . . disintegrating and out of balance yet still responding to patterning . . .[complex systems] self-organize into relatively stable states on a higher level of complexity than had previously existed, without a steering hand from outside.[10]

Change happens in between the extremes of stability and formlessness that is the edge of chaos. In the same way that we would never learn about the transformation of water into ice by always observing it at the same temperature, so too observing a waking dream continuously from the same perspective will preclude the necessary destabilization required to initiate change—a destabilization, or edge of chaos, that we have seen to be created by novel images, whether fairy tale frogs, air stewards on private jets, or fluorescent shopping bags caught up in the railings at the end of a street. However, as we have also seen, this destabilization should not go too far. Shocking novel images will stretch the dramatic tension of a waking dream beyond the edge of chaos, an overwhelm of thinking and feeling that will collapse the hypnagogic state.

The imaginal theory of change already sketched out and now confirmed and clarified by complexity theory is a fluid imaginal perception with a "dynamic equilibrium", able to navigate this middle ground between stability and complete chaos, between literalism on the one hand and flights of fantasy on the other. Too much order and change will not cross rigid boundaries; whereas, too much disorder will lack the cohesion to coalesce into the new. Only a sufficiently adaptable imagining that can enter the edge of chaos will be able to interrupt and transform the habitual patterning of self and world.

Emergence

The important point here is that changes made at the edge of chaos are self-organizing—in other words, changes that happen without any conscious direction, planning, or "steering hand from outside", all the things that complicated systems and the techniques of a mechanical imagination hold to be important. Complexity theory does not show us how to manufacture any particular change but rather, the necessary conditions required to initiate a self-organizing change from within the process of imagining itself. As can be seen in the often abrupt and unexpected developments of fairy tales:

> "I have had enough now," said the frog at last, "and as I am tired, you must carry me to your room, and make ready your silken bed, and we will lie down and go to sleep."
> Then the King's daughter began to weep, and was afraid of the cold frog, that nothing would satisfy him but he must sleep in her pretty clean bed.
> Now the King grew angry with her, saying, "That which

thou hast promised in thy time of necessity, must thou now perform."

So she picked up the frog with her finger and thumb, carried him upstairs and put him in a corner, and when she had lain down to sleep, he came creeping up, saying, "I am tired and want sleep as much as you; take me up, or I will tell your father."

Then she felt beside herself with rage, and picking him up, she threw him with all her strength against the wall, crying, "Now will you be quiet, you horrid frog!"

But as he fell, he ceased to be a frog, and became all at once a prince with beautiful kind eyes. And it came to pass that, with her father's consent, they became bride and bridegroom. And he told her how a wicked witch had bound him by her spells, and how no one but she alone could have released him, and that they two would go together to his father's kingdom.

A third advantage offered by complexity theory is the recognition of the unpredictability of imaginative experience in what is called "emergence". The highly novel possibility of sleeping with the yucky frog took the princess, no longer constrained by royal decorum, deeply into the edge of chaos, her anger breaking out in violence, smashing the frog into the wall, a fulsome participation and contact that did not result in the anticipated death of the frog but the entirely unexpected appearance of a prince!

In complexity theory, such spontaneous developments are emergent phenomena, "not reducible to the sum of the parts". In other words, the emergence of the prince is not just a rearrangement of the existing story elements but a reconfiguration into something entirely new and fresh.

The prince did not have a prior existence, waiting offstage for his cue to enter the story; yet the conventional view is that the prince is not a new development but merely a movement into conscious awareness of something that was already present in the unconscious. This is the mechanistic issue of the inner imagination understanding described in chapter 1: imagination as a zero-sum game, a collection of imaginal objects that can be moved around but not increased or destroyed. It is an understanding that pushes therapists towards mechanistic strategies to overcome "resistance" and provide a "counter-force" to adjust the "balance" of the psyche to allow this repressed unconscious material to enter awareness.

However, complexity theory tells us that this is not how change occurs. A more accurate way to picture imaginative change is to consider a waking dream or any other imaginal process metaphorically "as if" it were a pot of ingredients, such as a liquid mixture of flour, water, and yeast. Emergent images do not pre-exist in the same way that a loaf of bread does not have a prior existence. At best, these emergent images have a potential to exist, as does the loaf of bread within the mixture of ingredients; it is only through the agitation of entering into the edge of chaos (or the heat of an oven) that emergent images come into being.

As we have seen throughout this book, the imagery presented in psychotherapy and everyday life often arises in an unpredictable and spontaneous fashion—memories come back at odd moments; random details of a familiar street or person suddenly stand out as novel and strange; a solution to a difficult problem comes to mind when we are thinking about something else entirely—as does the narrative development of waking dreams take many unexpected twists and turns. And yet, this spontaneity of imagining, experientially apparent to the most cursory examination, is ignored or downplayed in conventional theories of imagination.

Set-piece imaginal techniques based on the assumption of a mechanical imagination suggest results that can be predicted and controlled; for example, focusing on an unfolding flower bud will teach us what is most beautiful in our lives; overcoming obstacles in a waking dream forest will strengthen our purpose and resolve; or simply imagining an improved version or "ideal model" of ourselves will make this so.

However, as discussed in chapter 7, the application of such techniques is no guarantee of the anticipated transformation of feeling, understanding, or behaviour. An unfolding flower bud might well highlight the ugliness of everyday life, not its beauty; failing to overcome the forest obstacles might create an anxious despair; and the ideal model of ourselves we conjure might only serve to painfully point out how far away and impossible that life seems. Much as we might enjoy the fantasy of predictive control, images do not change according to our wishes, as if by the simple flicking of a switch.

The lack of expected results from an imaginal technique is sometimes assumed to be due to a lack of focus and concentration. In other words, it is the imaginer not the technique that is at fault; if only we could try harder, success might be found. However, a fault of these techniques is an over-focus on achieving a particular outcome, inadvertently diverting the imaginer away from noticing those spontaneous imaginal developments that do indeed occur but which fail to fit into the pre-planned blueprint for change.

In the same way that we do not need to understand how telephones, light bulbs, or cars work in order to benefit from their effects, so, too, the assumption of imagination as a complicated machine pushes the imaginer towards the outcome of what is imagined and away from attending to the process of imagining itself. And yet, it is only in attending closely to this process that the actual rather than expected imaginal change will be noticed.

No matter how detailed the technique there will always be spontaneous imaginings along the way that deviate from generic formulae. Imaginal techniques are only a rough template to follow, "as if" we are setting the stage for a drama. The imaginal action that takes place upon the stage of a set-piece visualization or waking dream journey will always have unscripted elements, in the same way that each reader of the Frog Prince tale will see, feel, and hear a slightly different story.

If imagination is assumed to be complex system, then any one imaginal interaction, rather than having a singular and predictable cause and effect will be understood to have multiple and uncertain outcomes. As the Nobel prize–winning physicist Murray Gell-Mann has said, "The only valid model of a complex system is the system itself";[11] whereas, in a complicated or mechanical system, all the enclosed parts can be studied and a reliable model of how it works established: for example, knowing what speed and curvature of track will derail a steam train.

No matter how much time is spent observing a complex system, it will never be possible to accurately predict its behaviour. In the same way that the effect of a butterfly wing flap in Brazil on the weather in Texas cannot be forecast, so too the narrative developments of a waking dream cannot be predicted. However, what complexity theory does provide us with is a theoretical ground that values seemingly random, unexpected, or strange novel images as indicative of creative transformation, or what we can now call "emergence".

Emergence continues as the topic of the next Waking Dream chapter, where we will explore its practical applications across three aspects: synthesis, unpredictability, and the importance of butterfly-like small changes.

1. Rob Hopkins, *From What Is to What If: Unleashing the Power of Imagination to Create the Future We Want* (London: Chelsea Green Publishing, 2019), 51 (William Blake is quoted in a letter to Rev. John Tusler).

2. Steven Fesmire, *Ecological Imagination in Moral Education*, East and West. (Annales Philosophici, 2011), 20–34.

3. Jonathan Rowson, *The Moves That Matter: A Chess Grandmaster on the Game of Life* (London: Bloomsbury Publishing, 2019), 105 (Gregory Bateson quotation).

4. https://www.ecoself.net/which-self-needs-changing/

5. Robert Bosnak, *Embodiment: Creative Imagination in Medicine, Art and Travel* (Abbingdon, Oxon.: Routledge, 2007), 18.

6. I. Stewart, *Does God Play Dice?* (New York: Blackwell, 2002).

7. https://archive.org/stream/householdstoriesoogrim2/householdstoriesoogrim2_djvu.txt

8. Bruno Bettelheim, *The Uses of Enchantment: The Meaning and Importance of Fairy Tales* (New York: Penguin Press, 1991), 287–290.

9. Robert M. Galatzer-Levy, Psychoanalysis: *Notes from Forty Years of Chaos and Complexity Theory* (Abbingdon, Oxon.: Routledge, 2017), 225.

10. Robert Bosnak, *Embodiment: Creative Imagination in Medicine, Art and Travel* (Abbingdon, Oxon.: Routledge, 2007), 15–16.

11. https://blog.usejournal.com/7-differences-between-complex-and-complicated-fa44e0844606

Chapter 10

Waking Dreams No. 5 — Emerging

When complex form results from a process containing no model or blueprint of that form, we speak of "emergence" and call the resulting form "emergent."
—Robert M. Galatzer-Levy[1]

It is tempting to take complexity theory as a new and more complicated toolkit—and attempt to fit it within our existing approach to defining and solving problems.
—Jean Boulton[2]

I do not believe that we will ever arrive at an exhaustive list of operational conditions whose presence would definitely warrant the emergence of a given transpersonal or spiritual event.
—Jorge N. Ferrer[3]

The emergence from an edge of chaos in ecological imagining is now applied to imaginative change in waking dream practice. A perhaps obvious but nevertheless important point to make by way of introduction is that we shall not be taking emergence as a clever new technique to manipulate and control imagination. Emergence does not provide a neat formula for predictive change, and it will be shown that attempts to do so are fantasies of control that need to be relinquished in order to work with the subtleties of emergent phenomena.

This lack of a formulaic prescription to follow is reflected in the chapter structure, which departs from the established how-to three steps, everyday exercises, and therapy transcript examples. The absence of a three-step plan does not mean there is nothing to be done, however. In the same way as a white-water rafter is unable to plot a direct course through rapids but nevertheless engages with river turbulence rather than go with the flow, so too does a waking dreamer actively participate within the dramatic tension of an imaginative edge of chaos. To do so, what is needed is the ability to recognize emergence when it does occur.

The chapter therefore describes the qualities of emergence across three related aspects: synthesis, unpredictability, and small changes, each of which will be shown to provide an alternative to the three aspects of mechanical change presented in chapter 7: reductionism, malfunction, and determinism. Practical strategies and considerations to better notice emergent narrative developments will be related to examples from earlier Waking Dream chapters, where the application of complexity theory will be shown to further clarify the image-centric approach already established throughout the book.

Emergence No. 1: Synthesis

A first aspect of emergence is synthesis: the coming together of all the parts of a complex system to form a connected whole on a new level of complexity. A simple, illustrative example of emergence from synthesis is walking. If one leg is isolated from the other, we can only hop, which is something but not great; we can move much more easily by bringing both legs together, with the resultant walking motion being more than just a stronger hop. To walk is a qualitatively higher-order movement, an emergence of something new from the synthesis of both legs working together.

Of course, this is a simplification. Walking is more than just a synthesis of two legs. To walk involves the whole bodily system: a synthesis of muscle and bone, brain and nervous system, heart and lungs, and so on. To walk also includes the coordination of the bodily system with the surrounding environment, in countless micro adjustments of foot, ankle, and leg; sight, hearing, and balance; with the shifting surface textures, gradients, and obstacles. Further still, to walk is also a synthesis of the psychological functions: feeling and thinking, memories of the past, anticipations of the future: for example, in the way a particular path, running beneath the shade of some beech trees, evokes a mood of introspection, slowing the pace of thinking, and perhaps reminding us of a similar place and a wondering into the future, as to when we might return to this spot again. As ever more elements of the complex whole are included, it becomes apparent that this synthesis is not just about walking but also equally one of imagining.

The practice of waking dreams presented in this book has emphasized synthesis from the start. In chapter 1, imagination was presented as a synthetic function, a weaving together of all the senses and psychological faculties. This was then developed in chapter 2 into a description of the hypnagogic state required for waking dreams as a bringing together of the various imaginal sensations of sight, hearing, touch, and so on, with the imaginal feeling and thinking responses evoked by them, such that the waking dreamer becomes embedded within an immersive imaginative experience. Chapters 3 and 4 then made explicit this synthesis of imagining as a place; that to imagine is to find oneself in a three-dimensional image environment, an imaginal terrain through which we can walk and run and jump.

A waking dream is always taken within the context of the complex whole as a perception-feeling-thought-action drama, a process of imagining maintained by an ongoing multidimensional synthesis of all the elements within the complex whole. Only when a sufficient number of these elements combine will the waking dream enter the edge of chaos, that tipping point of complexity where new narrative possibilities emerge. As the biologist Stuart Kauffman explains:

> When a network or system reaches the condition of combinatorial optimization, there is a "combinatorial explosion". This critical transition takes place at the tipping point where quantitative change suddenly leads to qualitative change.[4]

When a critical number of elements come together in a complex system, a "combinatorial explosion" results in the emergence of something new; this also happens in a waking dream, with the inclusion of novel images, those figural or stand-out images that add further complexity, initiating a movement into the edge of chaos—the dramatic tension or "tipping point" of maximum imaginative possibilities.

The new direction that emerges is not just a quantitative rearrangement of what existed already but a qualitative transformation of the whole system, as happened in the Waking Dream transcripts with the client Daphne, when the novel image of a private jet created an edge of chaos from which the subsequent movement (chapter 4), dialogue (chapter 6) and shapeshifting (chapter 8) can now be seen as emergent phenomena.

The first strategy to facilitate emergence in a waking dream is therefore to approach the imagery as a synthesis, or coming together, of all the various elements within it. What matters is the participation and networking of relationships among all the images as an ecosystem, a strategy that is in critical contrast to those conventional waking dream approaches that feature analytical reductionism, the first of the three aspects of a mechanical understanding of imaginal change described in chapter 7.

While synthesis seeks to bring together ever more elements of a waking dream, reductionism moves in the opposite direction, simplifying a waking dream into its constituent part-images and treating each in isolation. It is a reductionism that can take one or other of the following directions, by focusing upon:

1 a single image-part, to the exclusion of the wider network of relations of which it is only one element;

2 the waking dreamer's feeling or thinking responses, to the neglect of continuing to attend to the sensory details of the imaginal environment;

3 the waking dreamer's thoughts, associations, and interpretations about the imagery.

In the same way that a single piece of a jigsaw will rarely help establish the whole picture, a narrow focus upon either a part-image, a feeling/thinking response, or a thinking-about association will undermine the synthesis of imaginal elements required to maintain the hypnagogic state.

While the insights arrived at by this close analytical study—for example, that a fear (feeling response) of a witch character (part-image) is symbolic of an uneasy relationship to anger and assertion (interpretation)—might be of interest, they will necessarily be dependent upon a separation from the immediacy of imaginative experience within the process of imagining. This is why such interpretations alone rarely lead to deep and lasting change. Isolated ideas about image-parts are not transformative because the lasting qualitative change that is emergence requires a combinatory optimization of all the parts of the system: a synthesis of imaginal sensation, feeling, and thinking.

Emergence No. 2: Unpredictability

A second aspect of emergence is its unpredictability. The synthesis of imagining results in a change process that does not proceed by simple cause-and-effect rules but appears all of a sudden, in an unexpected fashion.

In a complicated mechanical system (see chapter 9), change is linear and can be predicted. For example, the temperature of water in a kettle will rise in direct proportion to the rate of heat applied; the more powerful the kettle, the faster the water will come to the boil, and if the start temperature of the water is taken as a constant, then manufacturers can promise how long it will take for any given kettle to boil water.

In complex systems, emergent change is nonlinear, or unpredictable. For example, a seed planted in the ground will emerge into a tree, but how high it grows and the number and shape of its branches cannot be predetermined; a drop of condensation will eventually slide down a windowpane, but exactly when it begins to fall and what path it will take is uncertain; even the process of learning to walk will unfold in an unpredictable fashion, each child navigating a unique course.

The reason for all this unpredictability is because it is impossible to draw a line around a complex system and accurately model all the interactions among its component parts. How a tree grows will depend on soil, wind, sunshine, and rain created by conditions far beyond the tree itself; drops of condensation will fall in relationship to window and room temperatures, air currents, and vibrations caused by footsteps, trucks, and television sets; learning to walk will vary depending upon complex genetic, nutritional, environmental, and educational elements. As with trees, drops of condensation, and learning to walk, so too, narrative developments in waking dreams will emerge in sudden and unpredictable transformations. As the psychoanalyst Galatzer-Levy writes:

> Nonlinear thinking transformed the way we think about how systems evolve from an image of smooth transitions to one ordinarily involving radical jumps in transformations . . .[5]

No two waking dreams will emerge in the same fashion. While generic themes and outcomes can be recognized, the granular detail of each waking dream will emerge by way of irregular and unexpected "radical jumps". Even if the immediate focus of a waking dream is clear—for example, walking across a room or dialoguing with an imaginal character—the novel images by which these explorations emerge will be a unique journey that cannot be foreseen or pre-planned. We just don't know what will happen next.

A second strategy to facilitate emergence in a waking dream is therefore to expect the unexpected, so as to best notice the novel and irregular directions emergence takes, rather than only seeing the anticipated and familiar.

As a strategy this contrasts with the second aspect of a mechanical approach to imaginal change described in chapter 7, in which the part-images isolated by reductionism are treated as faulty or malfunctioning components in need of repair; in other words, the novel and strange are corrected to the anticipated and expected. In a waking dream as a complex system, quirky and unusual novel images are not a sign of brokenness but that which leads the way to unpredictable transformative possibilities. As psychosynthesis therapist Diana Whitmore writes:

> Problems and obstacles are seen not as pathological states
> to be eliminated but rather as creative opportunities.[6]

To expect the unexpected requires an openness towards situations, movements, behaviours, ideas, and feelings that confound habitual expectations, which can be exciting but also a bit scary. Too much unpredictability can result in an anxious avoidance of the new and imagining only what is expected and familiar, which will mean little or no change process. The important point here is to have some but not too much unpredictability, working within the edge-of-chaos tension that exists in between the overwhelm of the new and habitual familiarity. As Galatzer-Levy writes:

> New learning occurs . . . on the edge of chaos, between the twin dangers of stagnation and disorganization. This suggests that during a period of development, we would expect not to see an orderly unfolding of preprogrammed structures but, instead, periods of relative disorganization. Insofar as there is an underlying programme, it would be expected to be an arrangement designed to create a situation at the edge of chaos.[7]

Fantasy imagining, as introduced in chapter 1 and considered throughout the book, is by definition an avoidance of the edge of chaos. It is an imagining that imposes a predictable structure onto waking dream imagery, filtering from awareness any novel images that might lead to emergent developments so as to protect the egoic identity of the waking dreamer. The result is a waking dream that merely reconfirms pre-existing notions, feelings, and ways of being rather than exploring the new.

The opening sequence of the waking dream transcript in chapter 2 is an example of how fantasy imagining avoids unpredictability. The entry-point scene, sitting in an airplane, is initially described by the client Daphne as "pleasant" and "relaxed" and "privileged". There is nothing in the scene of a disturbing or unpredictable nature for quite some time, which allowed a safety to establish the hypnagogic state. Only in the next section of the transcript, in chapter 4, when Daphne is invited to look further, does she notice the unpredictability of her situation:

> Th: As you look around what stands out for you? What is most interesting?
>
> Cl: The veneer mahogany interior.
>
> Th: What does it look like?
>
> Cl: It's very shiny. It runs all around the lower half of the cabin. Oh, my gosh, it's a private jet! It's quite small. Like the ones you see in movies!
>
> Th: Is there anything else catching your attention?
>
> Cl: Yes! The other passengers are very well dressed, like business people. No-one is talking. It's a subdued atmosphere.
>
> Th: A subdued atmosphere.
>
> Cl: [*Pause*] It feels like there's been a mistake. I can't afford this kind of ticket. I'm not meant to be here.

Fantasy imagining is always a matter of degree. The initial airplane scene is a fantasy imagining in that it is not the whole story. Daphne did not notice until prompted that the airplane is a private jet, a novel image that took her into the uncertainty of the edge of chaos. Much of this book has already considered how best to work with the limitations of fantasy imagining. The following sub-strategies of "waking dream structure" and "imaginal attention" make this approach explicit with regard to facilitating the unpredictability of emergence.

Waking Dream Structure

Emergence is dependent upon being able to adjust the direction of a waking dream in response to novel images. The entirely unstructured, or spontaneous, approach taken across the Waking Dream chapter transcripts with Daphne has allowed a demonstration of how to follow the narrative developments created by novel images. Conventional approaches to waking dreams often impose a pre-planned structure onto the imagery, beginning with a generic entry point, such as a meadow or doorway (see chapter 2), then following a set-piece narrative of obstacles to overcome, characters to meet, and destinations to achieve.

The imaginal theory of change in these pre-planned waking dreams is a mechanical, or linear, one. The assumption is that exposure to symbolic imagery—sunshine, a wise being, or the ascent of a mountain—will result in a cause-and-effect transformation (see the "climbing a mountain" example in chapter 7). This assumption of linear change, especially when it has a set outcome or goal (developing the will, cultivating love, overcoming addictions, and so on) will act against noticing nonlinear developments. Imaginal attention is focused upon pre-planned imagery to the neglect of unpredictable novel images that do not fit neatly into the expected narrative formulae, a danger of which is a collusion and further enhancement of fantasy imagining and a waking dream that feels forced or made up.

A nonlinear theory of imaginal change recognizes that any pre-planned waking dream is really only a rough framework within which spontaneous emergence takes place, a stage upon which the real and unpredictable drama takes place. As psychoanalyst Galatzer-Levy writes: "The nonlinear . . . suggests a shift of analytic attention away from steps along a developmental line to the processes active in development itself."[8] In other words, an emphasis on the process of imagining rather than the successful reimagining of a structured content will be what best facilitates emergence.

Imaginal Attention

A sustained and refined imaginal attention will be what best notices the sudden, unexpected and strange novel developments at the edge of chaos. The three aspects of imagination presented across chapters 1, 3, and 5, alongside their practical application in chapters 2, 4, and 6, have shown how this imaginal attention can be developed.

Embodied imagination—a careful attention to embodied sensory experience; that is, the sights, sounds, touch, and so forth of the imaginal environment—will be important in order to counteract the emphasis upon subjective feeling and thinking of fantasy imagining that leads to the perception of what is expected rather than what is. For example, after noticing the private jet novel image, the next three therapist interventions directed Daphne towards sensory imaginal attention:

> Th: Can you focus on the imagery. What is happening on the airplane? What do you notice?
>
> Th: Can you hear the voices?
>
> Th: Not far away, behind you. How far?

Immersive Imagination—the slowing down of the pace of a waking dream—will assist in noticing novel images, counteracting the speed of fantasy imagining that allows it to rush past the strange and unfamiliar. This can be seen in the steady, unrushed treatment throughout the Waking Dream transcript with Daphne, which, as described in chapter 4, is more akin to the "slow burn of art-house cinema than the exciting narrative developments of an action movie".

Animistic Imagination—an animistic imagining of waking dream characters, places, and things as living beings—will grant them an autonomous otherness that confounds the objectification and control of fantasy imagining, an empathic stance that gets beneath surface appearances and into the moods and motivations of the imagery. For example, in chapter 6, the dialogue is built upon a careful imaginal attention to what is being communicated by the air steward novel image:

> Th: And what do you take from his expression?
>
> Cl: He's got this air of expectancy.
>
> Th: How can you tell?
>
> Cl: He's looking right at me. His eyebrows are raised slightly.

Th: And what is that expression telling you?

Cl: He knows I'm not meant to be here, that there's been a mistake.

A sensuous, patient, and empathic imaginal attention will best be able to both tolerate and follow the unpredictability of emergence beyond the limitations of the egoic-personality and fantasy imagination.

Emergence No 3: Small Changes

A third aspect to emergence is its sensitivity to small changes. Pictured famously as "the butterfly effect", complexity theory describes how a chain of consequences set in motion by something small and inconsequential—for example, the flap of a butterfly's wings in Brazil—can culminate in significant change, such as a tornado thousands of miles away in Texas. A complex system at the edge of chaos is understood to have multiple feedback loops that can quickly amplify and enhance even the tiniest of changes in one part of the system. Put simply, small changes in complex system can lead to large-scale consequences. As organizational consultant Sonja Blignaut writes:

> Outputs are not proportional or linearly related to inputs; small changes in one part of the system can cause sudden and unexpected outputs in other parts of the system or even system-wide reorganization.[9]

The recognition of this third aspect of emergence transformed the understanding of change in contemporary science. No longer assuming large-scale forces were needed to create significant change, scientists set about studying the world with fresh eyes.

An early topic of study illustrative of small-change emergence was the flocking behaviour of birds, such as happens during the winter months, when hundreds of starlings come together and create swirling aerial ballets across the evening skies called murmurations.

This flocking behaviour was computer-simulated in 1987, using a programme that tracked the movements of "boids" (short for "bird-oid object") according to three basic rules: steer to maintain set distance from local boids (separation), steer towards average heading of local boids (alignment), and steer towards average position of local boids (cohesion).[10] On a computer screen, the digital boids displayed the same flocking behaviour as birds in the natural world. Small-scale adjustments in the direction and speed of just one boid rippled through the entire flock, as successively ever further-away boids accordingly adjusted flight path and speed, which in turn then fedback to the first boid, which made further adjustments, and so on.

The macro-level effect was out of all proportion to the innumerable micro-manoeuvres made by individual boids and was considered an emergent behaviour characteristic of all complex systems at the edge of chaos. A third strategy to facilitate emergence in waking dreams is then to focus on the transformative effects of small changes.

A small-change strategy is once again not an entirely new approach. The process of imagining has been shown to depend upon following the many small-scale happenings that constitute the fabric of a waking dream: colours, shapes, and sounds; glances and gestures; words and pauses; fleeting feelings and thoughts.

The disproportionately emergent effects of these seemingly undramatic and small details have been demonstrated many times in the waking dream transcript with Daphne. In chapter 4, it was the veneer mahogany interior of the airplane; in chapter 6, the facial expression of the air steward; and in chapter 8, the hunched-up shoulders, hand grip, and muttering of the air steward. Each of these small image details, nested like a boid within a flock, interacting with the complex whole of the waking dream, led to the emergence of narrative developments: Daphne turned to look at the air steward, whom she then spoke with and subsequently shapeshifted into.

What can now be made explicit is how paradoxically ordinary and small-scale novel images can be, as also are the subtle plot developments they create. What makes for a novel image is the emotional response of the waking dreamer, rather than anything large, fantastic, and extraordinary in the image itself, as is the case in regular night dreams, in which the narrative story is more often shaped by changes in mood and atmosphere than any clearly defined boy-meets-girl-and-lives-happily-ever-after linear trajectory.

A small-change strategy further clarifies the difference between the image-centric approach presented in these Waking Dream chapters and determinism, the third aspect of a mechanical understanding of imaginal change described in chapter 7.

While a small change strategy rests upon a nonlinear conception of change in complex systems, determinism is a linear, cause-and-effect understanding of change in which "powerful" and "strong" images are assumed to be required to create imaginative transformation. With regards to facilitating emergence, the disadvantages of focusing on large-scale imagery—for example, travelling up a mountain path or soaking up the rays of a bright summer sun—is that attention is once again diverted from noticing the less dramatic and seemingly insignificant images that might more readily lead to emergent change.

1. Robert M. Galatzer-Levy, *Nonlinear Psychoanalysis: Notes from Forty Years of Chaos and Complexity Theory* (Abbingdon, Oxon.: Routledge, 2017), 82.

2. Jean G. Boulton, *Embracing Complexity: Strategic Perspectives for an Age of Turbulence* (Oxford University Press, 2015), 5.

3. Jorge N. Ferrer, *Revisioning Transpersonal Theory: A Participatory Vision of Human Spirituality* (State University of New York Press, 2001), 206–207.

4. Mark C. Taylor, *The Moment of Complexity: Emerging Network Culture* (University of Chicago Press, 2001), 147–148 (quoting Stuart Kauffman).

5. Robert M. Galatzer-Levy, *Nonlinear Psychoanalysis: Notes from Forty Years of Chaos and Complexity Theory* (Abbingdon, Oxon.: Routledge, 2017), 24.

6. Diana Whitmore, *Psychosynthesis Counselling in Action* (London: Sage Publications, 2000), 11.

7. Robert M. Galatzer-Levy, *Nonlinear Psychoanalysis: Notes from Forty Years of Chaos and Complexity Theory* (Abbingdon, Oxon.: Routledge, 2017), 81.

8. Robert M. Galatzer-Levy, *Nonlinear Psychoanalysis: Notes from Forty Years of Chaos and Complexity Theory* (Abbingdon, Oxon.: Routledge, 2017), 83.

9. https://blog.usejournal.com/7-differences-between-complex-and-complicated-fa44e0844606

10. https://en.wikipedia.org/wiki/Boids#

Chapter 11

Fractal Imagination

Life as a whole expresses itself as a force that cannot to be contained within any one part . . . . The things we call parts in every living being are so inseparable from the whole that they may be understood only in and with the whole.

—Goethe[1]

. . . fractal geometry inspires a whole different picture than splitting body from mind, isolating self from other, or wrenching inner from outer processes.

—Terry Marks-Tarlow[2]

If you like fractals, it is because you are made of them. If you can't stand fractals, it's because you can't stand yourself. It happens.

—Homes Smith[3]

"How you do sex is how you do the rest of your life."[4] This was one of the more memorable teachings I received in my psychotherapy training. Its immediate truth pulled the covers on my sex life, but also more broadly the innate pattern-making tendency of the psyche.

Not just sex but pretty much everything we think, feel, say, and do is a repeating pattern of core identities and ways of being deeply embedded within the psyche. Across such seemingly disparate contexts as sex, work, and dream life the same basic patterns can be recognized being played out again and again. And being able to notice and make these connections is a key psychotherapeutic skill, particularly for an image-centric approach. After all, patterns are nothing if not images.

In this chapter, we delve into the topic of imaginal patterning by continuing the exploration of metaphor within theories of imagination. Fractal geometry is shown to provide a metaphorical ground more closely aligned to the ecological complexity of human imagining than that of conventional approaches to patterning rooted in the mind-as-machine metaphor.

Fractal Geometry

The machines from which Freud derived his metaphors were themselves constructed from metaphors. The mechanical paradigm of the industrial age was built upon a metaphorical understanding of the world "as if" it were made of only straight lines, flat planes, perfect circles, and spheres. It was a linear world that had long since been the one and only geometry, stretching back 2,000 years to ancient Greece, where it was invented by Euclid, a geometric imagination so ubiquitous that its forms became metaphysical truths, the shapes a mathematician God had used to construct the natural world.

And yet, Euclidean geometry consists of abstract forms not at all found in nature. Trees are not straight lines, mountains are not isosceles triangles, and clouds are not perfect spheres. Nature is awash with ragged, wonky irregularity, a messy world that until very recently had largely been ignored by scientists. They had focused on the orderly problems their straight-line Euclidean geometry could solve; for example, the repeating uniformity of idealized wave forms rather than the turbulent crash of surf hitting the beach.

In this way, the industrial-age machines that Freud drew upon as a metaphorical ground for his psychological theories were a complicated but orderly simplification, rather than an accurate reflection of the real world, and it looked set to continue like this for another 2,000 years, when, in the 1970s, an entirely new geometric imagination emerged.

The new understanding was "fractal geometry". The new-fangled technology of portable computers starting to appear on scientists work benches allowed for the collection and processing of hitherto unprecedented amounts of data. It became possible to track multiple variables across a variety of time scales, such that problems previously overlooked for their complexity—long-range weather forecasts, beating human hearts, and city traffic jams—were now amenable to scientific study.

The results were surprising. The expansion of data revealed not more random chaos but an ordered patterning. On blinking green-blue monitors appeared wonderfully intricate repeating forms unlike anything seen before in linear Euclidean geometry, a pattern of repeating shapes that came to be known as "fractals". As the psychoanalyst Galatzer-Levy writes:

> Upon first examination the motions in systems may seem random and disorganized, but after many repetitions, we can see that they tend toward a particular pattern—not in the sense that they settle down but rather that the apparently wild shifts . . . represent tendencies to complex but representable patterns . . . of extraordinary beauty called fractals.[5]

Benoit Mandelbrot, the mathematician who coined the term "fractal" in 1975, described it as "a shape made of parts similar to the whole in some way".[6] Each fractal part is a self-similar miniature version of the larger pattern or whole, like a set of Russian dolls. The whole of the largest Russian doll is repeated in the successively smaller dolls within it, each of which is a nearly similar fractal shape and design as the preceding larger dolls. The large-scale fractal pattern is therefore repeated in the smaller scale parts within it, such that no matter what size of doll we pick, the same fractal pattern will be seen.

First discovered on computers, it was quickly understood that fractals are a natural-world phenomenon, hence they are also known as "the pictures of nature". It turns out that the building blocks of nature are not regular lines, cubes, and spheres but decidedly wonky and irregular fractal patterns.

One humble example is the fractal quality of broccoli, which repeats the same fractal shape on many different levels, from full head to tiny floret, which is also easily seen in cauliflowers, onions, pineapples, and ferns. Indeed, the branching growth of all plants and trees has a fractal structure. Crow's feet around the eyes and other areas of cracked skin also display a fractal patterning, as do the structures of the brain, lungs, circulatory, and nervous systems. Fractal patterns also make snowflakes, snail shells, river pathways, and the rippled surfaces of oceans, beaches, and deserts. Indeed, once we know what to look for, fractal patterns are difficult to avoid, and many disciplines have come to notice them, as organizational consultant Margaret Wheatley writes:

> From business forecasters and stock analysts who have observed a fractal quality to stock market behaviours, to physiologists who describe how the fractal quality of brain and lung tissues gives it far greater capacity, to architects who explain the beauty of buildings and towns as the repetition of harmonious patterns, fractals have entered the imagination and research of many disciplines.[7]

Fractal Imagination

The beauty of approaching imagination metaphorically "as if" it were fractal in structure is how intuitively close it feels to the nature of imaginative experience. In psychotherapy, for example, it is a well-recognized phenomenon that certain key moments, such as the first dream in classical psychoanalysis, present themes and styles of relating that are indicative of how the client goes about life in general. A fractal imagination both highlights and refines the ability to notice and work with this patterning, not just in stand-out moments but throughout every therapy session and into everyday life as well.

Any single piece of clinical material can be seen as a fractal image, reflective of patterns in the wider whole, and as each client only has one whole life, whatever level of enquiry taken will usually arrive at the same or very similar fractal pattern. As the psychoanalyst Galatzer-Levy writes:

> Psychoanalytic data is highly self-similar . . . careful enough attention to the material of single hours, or even fragments of hours, commonly reveals the way in which patients approach and work out difficulties on a larger scale, inside and outside of analysis . . . a patient's interests and concerns and style is detectable in very small fragments of material because of . . . the self-similarity of the personality.[8]

Small-scale fractal images are nested within larger narrative arcs like a set of Russian dolls. Regardless of context and local conditions, the same basic fractal image can be seen repeating itself on various scales of magnitude, creating self-similar situations and relationships. This recognition allows for the central premise shared throughout this book: the same imaginal themes found in "eyes-closed" waking dreams are also evident in generic psychotherapy and everyday life as an ongoing "eyes-wide-open" waking dream.

Fractal Dream Example

To provide a detailed example of fractal imagination, we now consider a dream reported by Daphne, the client featured in the Waking Dream chapter transcripts. By considering similarities between the dream and her everyday life across two scales of fractal attention— life context[9] and time period[10]—the basic template of the fractal image within not just the dream but across the whole of Daphne's life is slowly revealed. The dream is first summarized and then followed with a transcript of Daphne's description of fractal scales of attention.

The Dream

I am swimming in the Mediterranean Sea. It is a warm, bright, sunny day, and the water is a pure, clean, turquoise blue. The water is not busy. There are others swimming, but they are not close to me. There is a small cruise boat anchored nearby. There are people standing up in the boat, talking and relaxing. I'm enjoying floating around and soaking up the sun. Something in me decides to swim down underwater. I start pulling down through the water with strong strokes towards the bottom. The water gets darker, and a sense of urgency overtakes me as I see a newborn tiny baby trapped on the sea bed beneath bits of carpet and junk. I am anxious, and my heart is beating fast. I realize that there is too much junk for me to move on my own and there is no one around to help. The baby is dying, and there is nothing I can do. All I can do is watch.

Notes on Fractal Similarities across Scales of Life Context

Here the surprise, anxiety, and frozen powerlessness within the dream can be seen as a fractal pattern evident in Daphne's description of multiple contexts in her current everyday life:

Self-self context; that is, as noticed in bodily sensations, feelings, and thoughts:

I am always quite jumpy and anxious. I never find it easy to leave upsetting thoughts, lay them aside, and just get on with it. But when the anxiety spikes, I just freeze. Sometimes I can't even talk.

Self-other context; that is, as noticed in relationships:

Interviews and even just filling in application forms are where I feel this most strongly at the moment. I can't help thinking that I'm being found wanting, that I'm not good enough for the job. And so, I tend to hesitate and clam up, which just makes it worse.

Self-world context; that is, as noticed in encounters with objects, places, physical tasks, and so on:

> When I check my emails in the morning, often I can't believe how many there are, and I just try to ignore them, which of course doesn't work. They prey on my mind, wearing me down with anxiety.

Notes on Fractal Similarities across Scales of Time

Here again, the surprise, anxiety, and frozen powerlessness can similarly be seen as a fractal pattern now traced across Daphne's narrative on the dimension of time, from recent micro-moments all the way back into childhood history.

Seconds and minutes scale: tiny moments, spontaneous reactions, remarks, gestures, and so on:

> That moment when I step into the interview room and shake hands with the interviewers. It starts right there. I'm already in a panic. I'm already struggling to speak.

Hour long scale:

> The waking dream we did, the one about the private jet, is like this swimming dream, especially the initial burst of anxiety and the feeling like something is wrong.

Months-long scale:

> Since getting married, at home with my husband, I'm increasingly almost paranoid that he is angry with me for some reason, to which of course I don't say anything. I just wait for it all to go away.

Years-long/historical scale:

> Age 7: I was in a slot machine arcade with my mum, dad, and little brother. We were all wandering about and then an alarm went off. I thought it was the fire alarm. I got into an absolute panic and ran off and hid behind some bins in the car park.

> At birth: I was a premature baby, very weak, and had trouble being born. I nearly died and was put into an incubator.

Daphne easily recognized the dream as a fractal pattern present throughout her life. The same combination of anxious feeling, perception of threat, and a response of freezing and inaction were found across multiples scales of attention: in her relationship with herself, other people, and the world; as well as in tiny micro-moments, hour-, and month-long periods, as well as back into childhood history. And it is this ability to notice meaningful patterns across otherwise seemingly disconnected fragments of life experience that is a significant advantage of a fractal imagination approach. A second and related advantage is how working with a fractal rather than mechanical metaphor maintains therapy within the process of imagining.

Fractal Process and Mechanical Content

Patterns are images—images that are not, as we have seen throughout this book, discrete phenomena. Images are not confined to the visual seeing of optical pictures. To imagine requires a blend of all the senses and psychological faculties, a bringing together of seeing with hearing and touch, feeling and thinking, intuition and memory. As Roberto Assagioli writes:

> Imagination is a function which in itself is to some extent synthetic, since imagination can operate at several levels concurrently: those of sensation, feeling, thinking, and intuition.[11]

Imagination is a synthesis of many things. Images are a coming together of all the various faculties. The process of imagining can therefore not be properly understood in isolation. The quality of imaginal perception requires a holistic approach. And yet in the conventional approach to imaginal patterning, based on the assumptions of the mind-as-machine metaphor described in chapter 7, imagery is not approached as a whole but dismantled like an engine on a garage workbench. Instead of combining in synthesis, patterning is understood via a mechanistic reductionism that separates and simplifies.

In the above dream example, a reductionistic understanding of the pattern would first isolate the core experiences (the feeling of anxiety, belief of a threatening world, the frozen inability to act) and the key imaginal themes (the vulnerable baby or the anxious swimmer). These isolated dream parts would then be understood as being projected into the world, creating repetitively similar life situations and relationships.

It is a reductionistic approach to patterning that has long since stood the test of time and will be familiar to most if not all therapists for good reason: it does indeed reveal something of the nature of psychological patterning. However, from an image-centric perspective, this conventional approach has significant disadvantages.

If the therapeutic intention is to enhance and cultivate imaginative life, then a reductionistic reflection on patterning has little place in general, but particularly, during any kind of image-centric experiential work. The holistic synthesis of imaginal sensation, feeling, and thinking required to imagine is lost whenever a whole image is dismantled into separate image, feeling, and thinking parts. The reductionism of the mind-as-machine metaphor casts therapist and client alike in the role of mechanics, peering in at the particular feeling, thinking, and image parts of an inner imagination.

The effect is an emphasis upon the content of what has been imagined, rather than the process of how we imagine. It creates a retrospective and cognitive distance from the immediacy of imaginative experience, further exacerbated by the use of abstract analytical language, speaking of image fragments as "inner parts", "subpersonalities", and the "inner child". In summary, a reductionistic approach to imaginal patterning is a thinking-about images and their projections that eclipses the quality of perception required to imagine.

The significant opportunity of a fractal-imagination approach to patterning is one that not only maintains but allows for the cultivation of the process of imagining. The idea of "parts" in fractal geometry is of an entirely different order to the component parts of a machine. Fractal parts are not mechanical parts.

Recollect that the definition of a fractal is "a shape made of parts similar to the whole in some way". Spark plugs, fan belts, and piston heads are not fractal parts because they are dissimilar to the car engine of which they are a part; whereas, onion rings, fern leaves, and waking dreams are fractal parts because they have the same shape as the whole onion, fern plant, and everyday life of the waking dreamer. In this way, each fractal part, being self-similar to the whole, maintains rather than reduces the complexity of the whole.

A fractal-imagination approach to patterning is therefore one that avoids a reductive over-focus on any one element. For example, in the above dreamwork with Daphne, the various scales of fractal attention described an imaginal scene or memory in simple non-abstract everyday language, a description that offered a feeling-thinking-perception-drama. No one feeling, thought, or image fragment from the dream was taken in isolation as a central motif of the repeating pattern; instead, all the elements in the fractal pattern were approached simultaneously as an interconnected web of relationships on multiple levels, combining sense impressions with feelings, thoughts, and actions.

In this way, simply by inviting Daphne to notice the same imaginal themes found in the dream on multiple scales of attention elsewhere in her current and past life, the therapy session was maintained within the process of imagining. This allowed Daphne to maintain and cultivate the imaginal capacity to eventually experiment with new ways of being, as we shall soon see in the next Waking Dream chapter, where her case is again used to illustrate the further practical applications and principles of a fractal imagination.

1. Stephen Harrod Buhner, *Plant Intelligence and the Imaginal Realm* (Rochester, VT: Bear & Company/Inner Traditions, 2014), 72.

2. Terry Marks-Tarlow, *Psyche's Veil: Psychotherapy, Fractals and Complexity* (Abbingdon, Oxon.: Routledge, 2008),180.

3. Ibid., 178 (Homes Smith quote).

4. Angie Fee, *Sexuality and Gender* seminar (London: The Psychosynthesis Trust, circa 2004).

5. Robert M. Galatzer-Levy, *Nonlinear Psychoanalysis: Notes from Forty Years of Chaos and Complexity Theory* (Abbingdon, Oxon.: Routledge, 2017), 151–154.

6. Jens Feder, *Fractals* (Switzerland: Springer Science and Business Media, 2013), 11.

7. Margaret Wheatley, *Leadership and the New Science: Discovering Order in a Chaotic World* (Oakland, CA: Berrett-Koehler Publishers, 2006), 128.

8. Robert M. Galatzer-Levy, *Nonlinear Psychoanalysis: Notes from Forty Years of Chaos and Complexity Theory* (Abbingdon, Oxon.: Routledge, 2017), 159.

9. Terry Marks-Tarlow, *Psyche's Veil: Psychotherapy, Fractals and Complexity* (Abbingdon, Oxon.: Routledge, 2008), 180.

10. Robert M. Galatzer-Levy, *Nonlinear Psychoanalysis: Notes from Forty Years of Chaos and Complexity Theory* (Abbingdon, Oxon.: Routledge, 2017),157.

11. Roberto Assagioli, *Psychosynthesis: A Manual of Principles and Techniques* (London: Thorsons, 1993), 143.

Chapter 12

Waking Dreams No. 6 — Patterning

To find the whole in the part is to detect the magical en-
actment of psyche in the world.

—Terry Marks-Tarlow[1]

When you say you orient yourself to imagination with
whatever "presents" itself, you often start with what is
small and negligible. But as you follow the trail of hints,
you are led to larger and larger patterns.

—Paco Mitchell[2]

All good things come to an end, even waking dreams. Due to fading concentration or arriving at a natural conclusion, a decision
will be made to stop. Focus on the imagery is relaxed, and slowly
the hypnagogic state fades away. What happens next will deter-
mine the extent to which the imaginative potential of the waking
dream is further realized.

Broadly there are three possible responses to the completion
stage. The first and simplest is a non-response that allows us to sit
back and assume no further reflection or work is required. Given
that the waking dream imagery will have been healing and transformative on its own level, there is some merit to this approach;
however, a passive stance misses out on exploring the further potential of the waking dream, and it is often only employed as a re-
action to the more conventional second response: an
interpretation of what the imagery means.

This second response is essentially a rational translation of the
imagery into ideas and explanations that, as we have seen
throughout this book, allows imagining to be eclipsed by thinking.
This will effectively undo the quality of imaginal perception cultivated during the waking dream, yet, the pleasure of a neat inter-

pretation is hard to resist. Such is the predominance of the rational mind that it can seem counterintuitive to even suggest an alternative—after all, if we are not trying to figure out what the imagery means, then what's the point?

This chapter provides an answer to that question by imagining the possibilities of a third response: a non-interpretative application of the fractal imagination principles presented in the previous chapter. What we will discover is that by considering a waking dream as a template for a repeating fractal pattern, we can remain within an image-centric paradigm that allows imaginative potential to be not only maintained but further realized within the activity of images in everyday life.

Fractal Patterning: The Three Steps

As described in chapter 11, a fractal is a repeating image in which the shape of the whole is seen in the smaller parts within it. A classic example of a fractal is a set of nesting Russian dolls, where the largest Russian doll is repeated in successively smaller dolls; no matter what scale of attention we apply, the same or similar fractal image is found, from the largest to the smallest doll. From this, we can see that fractal patterning involves the recognition of a basic fractal shape or template repeating across multiple scales of magnification.

Before we continue with examples of fractal patterning in waking dreams, let's first look at the principles involved in recognizing them, as presented in the following three steps.

Step 1: Fractal Template

The first step is to clarify a template of the fractal pattern. This is largely done during the waking dream, but it can also be enhanced afterwards by choosing a particular moment or sequence of scenes and making a comprehensive description by asking a series of questions; for example: what is the landscape, room, furniture? What is the temperature, weather, and quality of light? Who is present? What are they wearing, doing, and saying? And from the imaginer's point of view, what feelings, thoughts, sensations, and actions are evoked? By bringing together all these elements and their interrelations, a fractal template is clarified. Only once this basic shape is established will it be possible to search for its repetition.

Step 2: Fractal Jumps

The second step moves beyond the waking dream imagery. By asking questions such as *Where have I seen this before? What feels familiar here?* we jump into repetitions of the fractal template. Often, these jumps will happen spontaneously, as a result of focusing upon the fractal template in step 1. It is therefore important to be open to the emergence of these repetitions of the pattern. The particular imaginal perception, behaviours, and relationships will be different, but it is usually not difficult to notice the underlying fractal themes, as from a fractal perspective, these jumps always land in the same place.

This spontaneous process can be encouraged by choosing "scales of attention" to reflect upon; for example: **Self-Self** (*Where have I felt, thought, and sensed like this before?*); **Self-Other** (*In what relationships have I seen this before?*); **Self-World** (*In what activities or perceptions have I seen this before?*); and **Time** (*In what micro-moments, hours, months, and past memories have I seen this before?*).

Step 3: Fractal Intricacy

The third step refines the scale of fractal attention. This happens over a period of time, repeating steps 1 and 2 in an iterative cycle, focusing on one of the fractal jumps, describing it ever more fully and then noticing further fractal jumps, and so on. The details of the fractal template becoming evident on ever more intricate scales of attention: in more subtle perceptions, feelings, thoughts, and behaviours; and in an ever descending time scale from hours down to minutes, until the fractal pattern becomes a lived experience in the moment that it is happening, as we shall see shortly in the waking dream examples.

Waking Dream Patterning in Everyday Life

The following exercise works through the three steps of fractal patterning as an "eyes-wide-open" waking dream. The first requirement is to take a walk and be on the lookout for a novel image, something striking and unusual that grabs our attention. Ideally, this novel image will be in the form of an object that we can pick up and use to work through the three steps; however, if this is not possible, something small from nearby that is reminiscent of the object will suffice. With the object before us, we then work through the instructions below to establish the fractal pattern. Each step is illustrated with a brief example.

Exercise 12.1 Found Fractal Object

Step 1: Fractal Template

Clarify the initial fractal template by describing in detail the scene around the novel object and the story of its discovery:

- What is the object? What is its size, shape, colour, texture, weight, and so on?

- Where was it found? What was the surrounding landscape, weather, quality of light, and so on?

- Who else was there? What other persons or creatures? What were they doing?

- How was it found? What drew you towards it?

- How did it make you think, feel, and move?

On his way to work one morning, Joe came across a caterpillar in distress. A wriggly green one, slap bang in the middle of the pavement, in imminent danger of being squished by commuters pouring out of the train station entrance. Anxious to avert disaster, he reached down to gently pick it up and transfer it to safety in some nearby shrubbery, only to realize that it was just a curled-up leaf gently rocking in the breeze.

Step 2: Fractal Jumps

Continue to hold in mind the fractal template described above and "jump" to self-similar fractal themes across various contexts and time scales elsewhere in your life. This might happen spontaneously and/or can be prompted by the following questions:

- What is familiar about these feelings and thoughts?

- What other persons or relationships does it remind you?

- Where else do you find yourself in this situation? What place or activity?

- When has this happened before—across years, hours, minutes, and micro-moments?

Joe noticed the same fractal pattern later at work, not with a caterpillar this time but with an e-mail. He read it quickly and knew right away that something needed to be done. Other people in the organization needed his urgent help or bad things were going to happen. He anxiously fired off a quick succession of e-mails offering his support and advice, only to realize a few hours later that he had misread the initial e-mail and really there was no need to panic at all.

Step 3: Fractal Intricacy

Continue to reflect on the fractal pattern over a period of time. Place the object in a prominent position where it will be noticed as a reminder of the pattern. Spend some time with the object each day. Hold it in your hands, and turn it over slowly. Be curious and receptive to the fractal pattern revealing itself on ever finer scales of attention and as lived in-the-moment experience. Talk about it in therapy or with a friend. Perhaps journal around the connections and links that come up.

Joe came to notice that his e-mail panic was a repeating pattern. Step 3 helped him to refine the time scale upon which he noticed the pattern. First, he came to recognize his overanxious response after writing his emails but before receiving any replies. Second, he came to recognize the pattern while writing the panicked e-mail, such that he did not need to send it. And third, a further refinement occurred as he noticed the pattern even earlier upon reading through his inbox of e-mails and before he had even written a word.

Waking Dream Patterning in Psychotherapy

The transcript below shows the three steps of fractal patterning in the continuation of my work Th: with the client Daphne Cl: featured across these Waking Dream chapters.

Step 1 demonstrates a successive clarification of the fractal template across three scales of attention: the fractal image is initially noticed on a tiny scale in spoken metaphor, which is developed into a micro-story that is then used as an entry point for a waking dream. Step 2 is accomplished through the work done upon completion of the waking dream to recognize the fractal pattern elsewhere in the therapy and within Daphne's everyday life, past and present. Step 3 shows a refinement of the fractal pattern within lived awareness, a development that subsequently allowed Daphne to complete this period of psychotherapy.

Step 1: Fractal Template

The transcript joins the work with Daphne three months on from the airplane waking dream transcribed in chapters 2, 4, 6, and 8. Daphne continued to be concerned with her anxiety levels but the focus had now moved on to include angry outbursts and arguments with her husband. At first, Daphne had assumed this to be a temporary aberration of her character, brought on by the stresses of job hunting; however, the arguments had continued and grown fiercer until she barely recognized herself anymore. Fifteen minutes into a session one morning, Daphne was reporting another of these arguments, when her tone suddenly became pleading, "He kept picking at me, and I just . . . you know?"

Her husband had not literally picked at her; the arguments were not physical. Daphne was speaking in metaphor, a way of imagining one thing "as if" it were another. The simple, sensory, and known experience of being "picked at" helped her convey something of the newfound strangeness in the arguments with her husband. Several other metaphors had already been mentioned—"fenced in", "a bit deflated", "going around the bend"—but these had been spoken in a neutral way as habitual turns of phrase. "Picking at me" had stood out in its pleading verbal tone and how she had accompanied it with gouging gestures against her forearm. It felt like a cry from the heart, an opening into her psychological life. Rather than letting it pass by, I simply reflected back:

Th: Picking at you?

Cl: Yeah, cutting into me with all these questions.

Th: Cutting into you?

Cl: He just kept coming at me, cutting me open, as if I was being operated on or something.

Th: Like in an operation?

Cl: Exactly—strapped down, with no way to move.

The initial metaphorical phrase had elaborated into a micro-story. "Picking at me" now had a setting with characters and a dramatic tension between them. A common strategy at this point would have been to reflect upon the characters in the story as sub-personalities, imaginal people symbolic of different parts of Daphne's psychological life: the vulnerable and defenceless patient as a Victim subpersonality and the mad surgeon as a Critic or Abuser subpersonality; however, a subpersonality approach would have been a theoretical simplification of the imagery, a reductionism of the complex whole into its component parts. In order to clarify the fractal template, we needed more not less complexity. I therefore proceeded by working with the operating room micro-story as an entry point to an "eyes-wide-open" waking dream, maintaining the session within the process of imagining,

Th: Okay, can you tell me a bit more as you lie there strapped down? What else do you see?

Cl: An operating theatre. Shiny metal. Lots of lights.

Th: A really bright space.

Cl: Yeah.

Th: How high is the ceiling above you?

Cl: It seems very high, but I can't see it because of the bright lights.

Th: And how far away are the walls of the theatre?"

Cl: About 3 metres away on either side. Green tiled walls.

Th: A big space. And what's the temperature? Are you hot or cold?

Cl: Hot, too warm, but I've only got a thin sheet covering me.

[Until this point, I had ignored the surgeon/husband character to allow sufficient safety for Daphne to further enter into the waking dream. Now that the hypn-

agogic state seemed well established, making sure to use the neutral "he" to match Daphne's language, rather than the "husband" and "surgeon" names from my parallel imagery, I simply asked:]

Th: And, where is he?

Cl: Right there beside me, preparing his instruments. I can hear them clinking around in a metal tray.

Th: And is he looking at you?

Cl: I can't tell. His face is in shadow from the lights. [*She swallowed hard.*]

Th: How is that to be there, strapped down like that?

[I wanted to include Daphne's obvious strength of feeling, weaving it alongside imaginal attention on the surrounding scene.]

Cl: Awful, just awful. I want to scream out in anger, but I can't. Like my body is anesthetized.

The successive elaboration of the fractal template from metaphor to micro-story to waking dream completed stage 1.

Step 2: Fractal Jumps

On completion of the waking dream, fractal jumps further established the repetition of the fractal template. Previous work had already laid the foundations for historical-scale jumps. Most obviously, the near death of Daphne's premature birth and subsequent isolation in an incubator showed the fractal pattern of threat, anxiety, and frozen inactivity. Also, her anxious father had indeed "picked at" her throughout her formative years, with cynical statements and accusatory questions that had caused Daphne to freeze with the fear and unexpressed anger she felt towards him—the same anger she felt unable to express towards the surgeon in the "operating theatre" waking dream.

It was clear from this early childhood history that being "operated upon" and "picked at" had once been an accurate imaginal perception; however, it had long since congealed into a habitual fantasy imagining (see chapter 1) or dead metaphor (see chapter 7), a repetitive reconfirmation of pre-existing notions that left Daphne trapped within the psychological atmosphere of a threatening world in which she felt powerless to act.

It was therefore not difficult to help Daphne recognize more recent fractal jumps to current "mad surgeons": the ongoing arguments with her husband; the anxiety spikes during job interviews; interactions with staff in shops, restaurants, and cafes; some old colleagues and friends; nighttime dreams; and several other waking dreams, including the one described in these Waking Dream chapters.

It seemed that no matter how considerate people were, Daphne was unable to reimagine and adapt to changing circumstances, continuing to find evidence to support her powerlessness in being "picked at"; however, bringing together and making connections among these fractal jumps allowed her a growing recognition of herself within the pattern, a recognition that led into the refinement of event and times scales of step 3.

Step 3: Fractal Intricacy

Two months on from the "operating theatre" waking dream, a significant opportunity for a refinement of the fractal pattern happened when the tension of the "picked at" story entered the therapeutic relationship between Daphne and me. Daphne had missed the previous week's therapy without informing me in advance and had thus incurred a charge. When this had previously happened, Daphne had promptly paid the fee, but this time she objected. She said that I was being "unfair", because she had "a good reason" for not being able to attend.

Her challenge was something new, and it surprised me. My first impulse was a defensive one. I wanted to push back by reminding her of the cancellation policy she had signed when she commenced therapy, but this felt like a lazy response—something else was going on. My defensive fantasy felt punitive, and then it dawned on me that by holding the payment boundary it was now me, in what therapists call "transference", who had become the Abuser Surgeon character to her Victim Patient identity. The tension over the cancellation payment was an in-the-moment repetition of the fractal pattern . . . although not quite.

The fractal pattern was self-similar but not exactly the same. The assertive expression of her anger towards me was something new. Until this point, the feeling of anger had indeed been emerging more strongly but was expressed only occasionally within some "eyes-closed" waking dreams. More often, the anger remained unexpressed, an aspect of her frozen powerlessness, as in the above "operating theatre" waking dream; now she was risking this out-of-character behaviour. It seemed important, therefore, to accept and encourage the imaginative possibilities currently at play.

To have acted upon my initially defensive impulse by reminding her of the contract would have been to overpower this emerging assertion, a needless repetition of the same old fractal pattern; instead, I continued the session by approaching her transference impression of me as an entry-point scene for an "eyes-wide-open" waking dream, a method previously described in chapter 4. I began with a simple reflection, which served to both show my acceptance of the transference and also to invite the further description of it needed for the first entering step:

Th: I'm being unfair somehow?

Cl: Yes, totally.

Th: How so?

Cl: Well there's the stupid rule, but its more about how you are enforcing it. It's like you don't care about why I missed the session.

Th: I see.

Cl: It's like you are not there for me today. You're being cold.

[It would have been very easy at this stage to offer an interpretation, to have explained away the tension as a fractal repetition; that really, I was still a good guy. Perhaps this would have been a relief for both of us, but also a lost opportunity. Thinking about the fractal would have been to step away from this fine-scaled study within the process of imagining.]

Th: And what's that like for you? How does it make you feel?

[This moved into entering step two: including her feeling and thinking responses.]

Cl: *[Daphne pauses, looks away from me. and says quietly]* It makes me angry.

Th: I'm being annoying?

Cl: Yeah.

Th: And how is it to tell me that?

[Her quiet voice did not seem angry, so I wanted to include this other layer of feeling.]

Cl: Well, it's good to say, but also scary.

Th: Scary. Okay, what's scary about it?

Cl: That you might not like it, that you might get even colder.

Th: Okay. I think I get it. My holding the line on payments feels punitive, like I'm not really there for you today. Which is annoying, right? But telling me that is a bit risky, as if it might mess things up between us even further.

[This long reflection is the third entering step, weaving together perception-feeling-thinking.]

Cl: Pretty much that's it, yeah.

Th: I'm picking at you.

[I could not resist mentioning the fractal, but made sure to keep it in the present tense as a description so as to keep away from it becoming an interpretation; that is, "This is another example of you feeling picked at," which would have taken us into thinking about the therapeutic relationship rather than imagining it from inside the process of imagining.]

Cl: Exactly.

Th: And is there anything else?

Cl: How do you mean?

Th: Well, if you were not so worried about being angry, what might you say or do?

[This moved us into the second of the exploring steps: considering possibilities.]

Cl: Ha! I'd tell you to stuff your cancellation policy! *[At which she gave me a huge grin, the expression of which was the third action step.]*

Th: Oh, yeah?

Cl: For sure. Stuff it. I'm not paying just because.

Th: And what is happening for you now? How is it to have told me that?

Cl: Pretty good, actually. Feels good.

Th: Not so scary after all then.

The waking dream continued by consolidating the result of the action step as a new entry-point scene and working through the three entering steps again. Daphne's perception of me had now altered. I remained colder than usual, but less so. Despite her fears of my becoming even colder it seemed the opposite had occurred. My continued acceptance and non-defensive interest had confounded her fractal expectations.

The slowed-down waking dream exploration of the transference allowed Daphne to become aware of the fractal pattern in the moment it was happening, a fine-grained fractal intricacy that allowed her perception to become informed, at least to some extent to begin with, by current experience rather than being an entirely habitual reimagining of the past, an imaginative malleability that held the metaphorical tension between similarity and difference. It was now "as if" I were (but not completely) the "abuser-surgeon" character.

The in-the-moment fractal intricacy and emerging assertion soon carried over into Daphne's everyday life beyond the consulting room. She increasingly noticed herself to be living within the midst of the fractal pattern as it was happening, an awareness of the repeating perception-action-feeling-thinking fractal complex from inside the process of imagining in which "picked at" was no longer the only way of seeing and feeling. Her husband was at times still annoying, and she continued to feel anxious in interviews, but it was now more "as if" she were an anesthetized patient (but not the same as). The fractal pattern was not completely eradicated, but her fine-grained attention meant that she no longer felt at the mercy of events and powerful others. She began to feel more confident. Her assertion and power continued to emerge. She felt safer rather than anxious, no longer frozen with fear.

The Therapist Role and Language

Use of the word "fractal" can, depending on context, either be an abstract analytical concept or an image; this is an important distinction for image-centric therapists to consider with respect to the style of language needed to deliver a fractal approach appropriately within waking dreams.

In previous Waking Dream chapters, we have noted that the therapist's language should avoid theoretical terms, such as "subpersonality" and "Inner Child"; instead, simple everyday language should be used to provide a detailed description of the imaginal environment and the response it evokes in the waking dreamer; for example, rather than an "Angry subpersonality", we have a frowning air steward with cold, serious eyes, mumbling under his breath. In this way, layers of connecting details within an encompassing image environment establish and maintain the hypnagogic state. This approach is now applied to the appropriate use of the term "fractal" across the three steps of patterning.

In step 1 (establishing the fractal template), use of the word "fractal" is not advised. The intensive focus within a single scale of attention provides little if any basis for using fractal as a descriptive term with the client. In the above example with Daphne, to have suggested during step 1 that "This surgery scene is what we call a fractal . . . it's the same imaginal template as happens to you in interviews" would have interrupted the immediacy of the imaginal process, undermining the quality of attention needed to maintain the hypnagogic state.

In the same way that analytical language turns images into ideas that inevitably lead to comparisons with what the imagery symbolizes, or represents—for example, when a Surgeon Abuser character is compared to a historical father—so too does using the word "fractal" introduce a comparative leap away from the immediacy of the unfolding waking dream narrative. The effect is to bypass further description and clarification of the fractal template in a premature rush into step 2, considering fractal jumps or repetitions of the waking dream imagery; hence, the notion of "fractal" remained a theoretical metaphor on my part as the therapist during step 1.

In steps 2 and 3, possibilities for sharing an explicit fractal approach with the client become possible. As described in chapter 11, fractals are understood to be a natural world phenomenon, sometimes being called "the pictures of nature". Fractal is therefore not just an abstract mathematical concept but also a descriptive term, in the same way that waves, echoes, and vibrations can be used theoretically but also as descriptions of naturally occurring phenomena. It is this descriptive function that provides a rationale for a judicious introduction of the language of fractals to the client—as an *experiential* rather than a *theoretical* metaphor.

In practice this will be done once fractal jumps have built up sufficient evidence of patterning, so that the introduction of fractals meets with a direct fit in experience across multiple scales of attention, rather than an abstraction that takes the client away from a single scale of attention, as in step 1. If the presentation of fractals is given alongside common examples from nature—clouds and mountain ranges, crystals and snowflakes, broccoli and onions—the resonance between this fractal patterning in nature and those in the client's life can stimulate further fractal jumps. In this way, fractals can be embraced explicitly as an intuitive and holistic approach to imaginative life.

In step 3, an explicit fractal approach can be helpful in addressing unreasonable expectations from the client of complete symptom removal. While the return of the fractal pattern to the same basic issues can be discouraging, the introduction of these patterns as "fractal" allows the client to see that the previously gross perceptions and behaviours of the pattern have, in step 3, become refined to much smaller and manageable symptoms.

The advantage of this approach is that progress is no longer viewed in an all-or-nothing way. One example might be the alcohol addict who, despite being sober continues to have addictive tendencies. On being introduced to fractals, they grow interested in gauging progress by noticing ever more intricate scales of attention in respect to the objects of craving (a bottle, a drink, a cake, a smile, and so on) and the length of the craving cycles (week-long benders, single-night binges, sober but thinking about drink all the time, then less and less, and so on). This attention towards the subtlety of patterning feeds back iteratively to drive further change.

1. Terry Marks-Tarlow, *Psyche's Veil: Psychotherapy, Fractals and Complexity* (Abbingdon, Oxon.: Routledge, 2008), 26.

2. Russell Lockhart and Paco Mitchell, *Dreams, Bones & the Future: A Dialogue* (Owl and Heron Press, 2015), 42.

Chapter 13

Transpersonal Imagination

"Transpersonal" multivalently acknowledges the sacred dimension of life dynamically moving beyond as well as within, through, and by way of the human person in a manner that is mutually transformative, complexly creative, opening to a fuller participation in the divine creativity that is the human person and the ever unfolding cosmos.

—Richard Tarnas[1]

This book began by asking three questions: What is imagination? How can we imagine more fully? Why would we want to? We have come a long way in pursuing this enquiry and establishing an image-centric understanding and approach. Until now, though, I have held back the transpersonal context within which this enquiry was originally conceived.

As mentioned in the introduction, the ideas and strategies presented here first began to take shape during my psychotherapy training in the psychosynthesis of Roberto Assagioli. Those familiar with psychosynthesis will have perhaps recognized this background influence; however, until this point, I have avoided an explicit treatment of the transpersonal philosophy, or framework, of psychosynthesis with respect to imagination and chosen instead to offer a jargon-free presentation for the general interest reader.

This concluding chapter now offers a suitable opportunity to pull back the curtain on this background influence as a way to bring together the various concepts and strategies presented thus far under the umbrella of a transpersonal (beyond-the-personal) imagination.

Transpersonal Psychotherapy

The Italian psychiatrist Roberto Assagioli began developing psychosynthesis in 1911. An early proponent of psychoanalysis, Assagioli valued Freud's insights but argued that they were incomplete.[2] In naming his new psychology "psychosynthesis", he sought to distinguish it from psychoanalysis. While the term "analysis" refers to the reductionism, or breaking down, of complex wholes, "synthesis" instead emphasized Assagioli's focus upon bringing together the disparate elements of the psyche into an ever increasing wholeness. As Assagioli said in interview:

> I never met Freud personally, but I corresponded with him, and he wrote to Jung expressing the hope that I would further the cause of psychoanalysis in Italy. But I soon became a heretic.[3]

Assagioli broke with Freud several years before Carl Jung but for similar reasons—both becoming "heretics" by refusing to accept Freud's reductionistic emphasis on childhood issues and a neglect of the wider potentials in human psychology. A forerunner of both humanistic and transpersonal psychology, Assagioli was among the first psychologists to move on from studying only the brokenness of human suffering to an enquiry into the creative, aesthetic, and spiritual experiences of healthy human potential.

Psychosynthesis applied insights from a fusion of Western psychology and Eastern religious traditions, validating heightened or altered states of consciousness, not as a regressive return to preegoic childlike oneness, as per Freud, but as indicative of coming into relationship with a source of wisdom and direction operating beyond the personality; hence, the coinage of "transpersonal" ("trans" meaning "beyond"). Here, psychosynthesis places the "personal self" (a centre of consciousness and will)[4] within a broad and expansive psychological context, effectively turning inside out common assumptions of a purely inner or intrapsychic psychology, granting validity to those moments of connection and belonging, as for example might happen on spending time in the countryside, talking with a good friend, or listening to music—moments that while perhaps not entirely objective are nevertheless not entirely subjective or inner experiences either.

In respect to our topic, Assagioli identified imagination as one of the modalities by which the individual or personal self finds a relationship to the transpersonal; a significant advance beyond the narrow focus in psychology upon feeling and thinking at that time.[5] Indeed, he considered imagination to be an equal psychological function to feeling, thinking, and sensing, positing a number of psychological laws that describe how we will find a related image within each thought or feeling or bodily sensation; a validation of imagining and its relationship to the other psychological functions that provides the theoretical basis for the plethora of image-based experiential techniques often applied in psychosynthesis psychotherapy.[6] And it was this foregrounding of imagination that, as mentioned in the introduction, had attracted me to choosing a psychosynthesis training over other orientations. I figured it might give me the clues to recover my imaginative life—that enchanted story-filled existence recalled from childhood, the remnants of which were fading with every passing year.

From the start, we were indeed visualizing, drawing, making masks, performing psychodrama, journaling, and talking about dreams. It was all very creative and exciting and fun. Which is perhaps why it took quite some time for me to realize that all this activity was having very little impact on the recovery of my imaginative life. Something important was missing.

The Imagination Imagined

The "something missing" in my psychosynthesis training was ironically a language that spoke to and validated imagining as a transpersonal experience.

In the psychosynthesis literature, characters of imagination were "inner figures" approached through an "inner programme" or "inner dialogue", resulting in an "inner integration".[7,8,9] Far from alluding to the activity of images in everyday life, this language seemed to limit imagining within the bounds of the personality.

And yet, when I looked beyond the theory, at what actually happened in therapy rooms, it was clear that something else was going on. Very often therapy involved a certain belief in the reality of an imagined character, not as an inner figure but as an imaginal presence in the world. Whether perceived in a teddy bear, a drawing exercise, or in a landscape of imagination during a waking dream, such figures were often dialogued with as if they were independent and autonomous others. It seemed that therapists and clients alike were comfortable with this activity of images in the world, in practice if not in theory.

I took advantage of a research project during my psychotherapy training to explore this gap between actual imaginal practice and theoretical understanding. The title of my project was "The Imagination Imagined".[10] It aimed to find out how a therapist's theoretical assumptions regarding imagination qualitatively shaped the client's imaginative experience. A series of interviews were conducted with psychosynthesis psychotherapists, a key part of which invited them to share how they might have responded to the following clinical situation, based upon a composite from my own practice:

> A client reports how he had been looking out a train window, more daydreaming than noticing the countryside slipping past, and how, on turning back into the carriage, he saw on the chair opposite him a little boy whom he recognized as his younger self, quietly sitting and looking back at him.
>
> The client knew it was not a physically present little boy, and yet it "did not feel made up" and had "a sort of reality".
>
> If we take it for granted that this client is psychologically stable, how might you have responded?

The results of the interviews fell broadly into two groups. In the first group, imagination was assumed to be a psychological interiority. The understanding of the "little boy" was as an internalization of the client's actual historical "little boy". What the client saw was a projection of a memory, a picture from childhood that properly lived inside him and was only momentarily cast out into the world. In other words, the "little boy" did not really belong on the chair; hence, this first group would have focused upon tracing down its origins in childhood events.

The first group would have offered this inner imagination understanding to the client in an unqualified manner, using terms such as "subpersonality" and "Inner Child" or the phrase "that child part of you" to describe and reflect upon the "little boy", all of which signposted a personal rather than a transpersonal imagining.

Of course, this language of inner figures and sub-parts, as we saw in chapters 1 and 7, is best understood as a metaphor. Images are only "as if" but not really inside us, and yet the idea of an inner imagination for this first group of interviewees was not just one story among many but a matter-of-fact reality. It was a way of speaking that, as we have seen throughout this book, was more than just an idea or theory but also active in shaping imaginative experience as a personal historical interiority.

I was not surprised that the first group of interviewees held this inner imagination theoretical position; as already mentioned, it was the only presentation I had found in the psychosynthesis literature. However, the second group of interviewees described an alternative way of working. In their response to the client, they would have avoided any abstract language, such as "Inner Child" or "subpersonality", as well as any search for the historical origins of the "little boy". Instead, these therapists described the importance of matching the client's language and using a simple non-jargonistic description of the experience that acknowledged the reality of the character for the client.

This second group was consciously avoiding inner imagination language. It was understood that such an approach undermined an experiential exploration, which these therapists valued highly, by moving the therapy towards a more interpretative and rational direction. One of the therapists in this group spoke of how it was "important that the client is connecting with their imaginal sense, rather than being a detective and tracking down something that happened in the past". Another suggested: "You step in and explore: what does he look like, how do you feel towards him?" In this way, far from diverting attention from the activity of images beyond the personal (in this case, the "little boy" on the train), its possibility was taken seriously and enhanced, an approach that I took as offering some ground for a transpersonal imagining.

The two groups were separated theoretically as well as methodologically. It was not just a clever language game. How these therapists understood imagination mattered. While none of the second group were able to succinctly describe an actual theoretical position on the reality or otherwise of the "little boy" image, they nevertheless all recognized there was more to it than the inner imagination understanding, which they took much more provisionally than the first group. In other words, the second group made a distinction between theory and practice rather than conflating them like the first group.

One therapist in the second group described this approach as an invitation for the client "to live more from the basis of a mythic realm than from the centralised ego". Another spoke of "a discussion of what makes the world a magical, meaningful place . . . which needs opened, validated, explored, so that the client can have it more consciously".

I concluded that it was their theoretical openness towards imagination that allowed this second group to convey an interest in the client's actual imaginative experience rather than squeezing the "little boy" into a narrow inner imagination belief system like the first group did.

So, what was going on? How could there be such a marked difference towards imagination between these two groups of psychotherapists, all of whom had been trained in the same psychosynthesis method? The pursuit of these questions led me to discover a tension between two competing stories within psychosynthesis, and much of transpersonal therapy besides.

Empiricism and Mysticism

A tension at the heart of psychosynthesis lies in a confusion over whether it is an empirical science or a mystical practice.

As mentioned earlier, in his conception of psychosynthesis Roberto Assagioli drew upon sources from both Western psychology and Eastern religion. This fusion of interests mirrored his background as both a medical doctor steeped in the empirical method and a classically educated scholar of Buddhism and Hinduism, as well as pre-modern western traditions such as kabbalah, alchemy, and esoteric Christianity. He therefore drew upon influences from both empirical science and what psychosynthesis writer Jean Hardy describes as his "mystical" interests. And it was in tracing the tensions between empiricism and mysticism in psychosynthesis that allowed me to understand the different approaches to imagination shown by the two groups of interviewees. As Jean Hardy writes:

> In asking about the origin of the ideas contained in psychosynthesis, and the nature of the knowledge that it embraces, it is necessary to examine the relationship of mystical to scientific knowledge, because that is the tension within psychosynthesis and indeed within any transpersonal psychology.[11]

Most clearly, there is the empirical scientific influence. Instead of inventing a new terminology, aligned to the experiential recognition of a truly beyond-the-personal psychology, Assagioli adopted the Freudian focus upon subjective inner experience. As we saw in chapter 7, Freud presented psychoanalysis as an internalization of the experimental methods of empiricism, the aim of which was to isolate the subjective bias of the scientist in order to better observe, predict, and control the objective world. In the same way scientists observed objects in the physical world, so too, Freud came to observe feelings, thoughts, and the imagery of dreams as psychological objects contained within human subjectivity. This framework of subject/object and inner/outer was simply inherited and built upon by transpersonal psychology. As transpersonal writer Jorge N. Ferrer writes, while the aesthetic, meditative, and spiritual experiences validated by transpersonal psychology essentially "collapse the distinction between subject and object",[12] most of the early transpersonal authors based their theory on unexamined "objectivist epistemological assumptions",[13] the consequence being that transpersonal phenomena were assumed to be located within human subjectivity:

> ... if the only valid knowledge was the empirical one, then the epistemic legitimacy of transpersonal studies had to be defined in terms of a "science of human experience", an "inner empiricism" . . . a "science of consciousness".[14]

From 1911, when he started writing about psychosynthesis, until the time of his death in 1974, the predominance of empirical science meant that in order to be taken seriously, Assagioli, alongside other emerging transpersonal psychologists, had to present his ideas as a bona-fide empirical science. He wrote that psychosynthesis could be "proven by direct experience", which had "full scientific value, in the broader sense".[15] While this scientific influence was made explicit, the mystical influences upon his thinking were downplayed for strategic reasons. Jean Hardy writes of how Assagioli deliberately chose not to mention his non-scientific influences because he "was determined that his work should pass muster and be accepted as a respectable scientific theory".[16] Indeed, he famously spoke of placing the mystical sources of his ideas behind a "wall of silence".[17]

What the modern era labelled as "mystical traditions", due to their lack of a clear separation between self and world, were repackaged by Assagioli in a language palatable to a contemporary audience. The experiential recognition of a beyond-the-personal psychology was conceived theoretically as an expansion or refinement of subjective consciousness rather than a movement beyond the confines of a personal "me", per se. Of course, this is not to dismiss the importance of the subjective within transpersonal experience. Jorge N. Ferrer clearly acknowledges this subjective dimension, but goes on to reject what he describes as "the anthropocentric, and ultimately egocentric, move to infer...that transpersonal phenomena are essentially human inner experiences".[18]

The presentation of transpersonal psychology as an inner experience, while perhaps historically necessary, is at best a simplification of beyond-the-personal phenomena. Below, four limitations arising from an empirical understanding of transpersonal psychotherapy generally, and psychosynthesis in particular, are briefly sketched out.

Dualistic

The empirical method assumes a neutral position somehow outside the experiences observed. As mentioned in chapter 7, this is the root metaphor for the original Freudian analyst, sitting out of sight from the patient and saying little "as if" a neutral and non-involved empirical observer—a dualism of therapist/client. And yet the language of inner empiricism is anything but neutral. As we have seen throughout this book, terms such as "subpersonality", "Inner-Child", and even the "unconscious", actively shape experience. As employed by the first group of interviewees, these terms were a lens through which they viewed the "little boy" clinical vignette, framing everything within dualistic categories such as inner/outer, subjective/objective, self/world, real/unreal.

Psychosynthesis writer John Firman writes of a "trouble in the soul of psychosynthesis" as the dualistic presentation by Assagioli of the "personal self" as a spiritual essence somehow above and beyond the vicissitudes of everyday life and the material world, entirely separate and distinct from the body, feelings, and mind.[19] This is a dualism that we can see in the following quote from Assagioli:

> In other words, one becomes a self who uses the body, the feeling apparatus and the mental abilities as tools, as instruments, in the same way as a car is the extension of a driver. . .[20]

Firman describes how this dualism of personal self/body-feelings-mind can lead to a spiritual persona or identification that actively avoids embodiment and all non-spiritual states, such as anger, grief, lust; the results of which will lie somewhere between a mild neurosis and an extreme alienation or dissociation. The first limitation of a dualistic approach is therefore a simplification and separation from an embodied participation within the joined-up complexity of transpersonal experience.

Rationalistic

The explicit usage of inner empirical language, such as "sub-personality" and "Inner Child", by the first group of interviewees described a rationalistic therapeutic enquiry of the "little boy" character. The "little boy" was assumed to be a symbolic representation of meanings to be found not in the imaginal encounter itself but in historical childhood events and related feeling-thinking states. As we have seen throughout this book, the effect of this analytical approach is a retrospective thinking-about causal reasons and explanations, which is once again a simplification and separation from the immediacy and meaningfulness of transpersonal phenomena.

The second group of interviewees avoided this rationalistic limitation by emphasizing simple descriptive rather than abstract analytical language. The "little boy" was approached experientially, as an image on its own level, rather than rationally as a puzzle to be solved. While this included the client's personal feelings, thoughts, and bodily sensations in response to the "little boy", the second group did not assume from this subjective perspective that the location of the "little boy" was within the client's psychological subjectivity. In this way, they were able to align themselves with the experiential beyond-the-personal phenomena of the "little boy".

Narcissistic

A further limitation of viewing transpersonal experiences as inner and subjective is an inadvertent self-inflation and narcissistic preoccupation with personal spiritual practices and attainments. As Jorge N. Ferrer writes:

> To draw transpersonal and spiritual phenomena out of the realm of inner experience is to pull them out of the domain where the ego believes itself sovereign and . . . thwarts to a large extent the illegitimate egoic appropriation of spirituality that I have called spiritual narcissism.[21]

Instead of seeking to build a relational bridge into the world of people, places, and things, transpersonal theory presented as an inner empiricism directs attention within, towards the cultivation of heightened states of consciousness. In psychosynthesis, a basis for this self-centred and narcissistic limitation can be seen in the emphasis Assagioli places upon personal control, as seen in his description of "disidentification", a core idea in psychosynthesis:

> We are dominated and controlled by everything with which our self becomes identified. We can dominate and control everything from which we disidentify ourselves.[22]

However, it is not difficult to see how a therapeutic goal of control and domination can easily lead to an exaggeration rather than a maturation of the habitual egoic self. As we saw with respect to the imagination in chapter 5, assumptions of control run the danger of turning transpersonal psychotherapy into an egocentric colonization project rather than a movement beyond the confines of the personal self, one that precludes or downplays the possibility suggested above, by one of the interviewees in the second group, of the "little boy" as an opportunity "to live more from the basis of a mythic realm than from the centralized ego".

Mechanistic

In conceiving of transpersonal experiences as an expansion of subjective consciousness, transpersonal psychology followed the Freudian maxim, "Where id was, there ego shall be."[23] In other words, the goal of therapy was to shine the light of consciousness into the darkness of the unconscious. The dark, unruly, irrational forces of the unconscious, or id, would be tamed by the rational ego.

As a way of thinking about psychology, there are many advantages to this framing, as attested by its continued usage. However, with frequent usage it can easily be mistaken for a literal truth rather than a metaphorical "as if" imagining. As we have seen, particularly in chapters 7 and 8, this leads to a theory of change that assumes personal transformation to be a revealing of what already exists, rather than the creation of something entirely new—a mechanical change in which experiences are theorized "as if" they were psychological parts that can be moved from unconscious into conscious awareness.

For example, the first group of interviewees assumed "the little boy" as a pre-existing inner figure that had become conscious, a return to the past rather than a stepping into the new, the limitation of which is the preclusion of other future-oriented possibilities, such as the often unpredictable and non-mechanical nature of change in actual, rather than just theoretical, therapeutic practice.

Despite these four limitations, the presentation of psychosynthesis as an empirical science has not managed to entirely conceal the implicit influence of Assagioli's mysticism. The second group of interviewees granted the "little boy" a status in the world and worked to explore the client's relationship with it in a manner not dissimilar to how Richard Tarnas describes pre-modern peoples as "emotionally, mystically, consequentially" participating and embedded in a world that was understood to be "speaking a symbolic language".[24] Whether buried within the written teachings of psychosynthesis, passed on by word of mouth, or simply rediscovered anew by each generation of therapists, an acknowledgement of the activity of images in everyday life does find a place in some, if not all, therapeutic practice.

The good news is that transpersonal psychotherapy no longer needs to keep its mysticism a secret. While an empirical world view continues to inform common-sense assumptions about how things are, contemporary scientists, psychologists, and philosophers are offering mainstream critiques of the radical separation between self and world inherent in the empirical method. In other words, empiricism is no longer hegemonic, and a more joined-up world view is emerging. As discussed in chapters 9 and 11, science now offers alternatives to empiricism, a conceptual renaissance within which many psychotherapists are challenging and going beyond the limitations of a one-person singular "me" psychology separated from an objective factual world.

If the transpersonal is no longer assumed to be an inner event, it can therefore find a language and theory more fully aligned to the nature of beyond-the-personal experience, one that acknowledges rather than denies the possibilities of Assagioli's mystical influences. It is a context that now allows for a re-imagining of transpersonal psychotherapy, releasing the hidden potential of its many image-based methods from the constraints of a strictly inner or intrapsychic approach.

A Transpersonal Imagination

Assagioli spoke of wanting to return soul to modern psychology.[25] In chapter 3, an equivalence between soul (as "a perspective rather than a substance" and the "middle ground between us and events") and imagination (as the "perception of images arising in between self and world") was established. It is therefore no great leap to now also point out a similar equivalence between transpersonal and imaginative experience.

By drawing upon a broadly conceived understanding of transpersonal, such as the one quoted at the head of this chapter as "dynamically moving beyond as well as within" and "opening to a fuller participation in the divine creativity that is the human person and the ever unfolding cosmos", we can see that transpersonal experience is more than an awakening to inner potential or the expansion of subjective consciousness. In the same way that this book has described how imaginative experience is not confined to inner experience but is present in the activity of images in everyday life, so too does a transpersonal psychology seek to contextualize the individual within the fabric of the surrounding world and encompassing cosmos.

Without seeking to collapse all distinctions, imagination can be characterized as transpersonal, and vice-versa. It's a similarity that now allows me to sketch out the characteristics of a transpersonal imagination dynamically moving beyond, as well as within, through, and by way of everyday relationships with people, places, and things; a joined-up imagining that allows us to consider those moments of connection and belonging that bring together rather than divide inner and outer, subject and object, self and world.

In chapter 1, the same four limitations of empiricism in transpersonal theory mentioned above (dualistic, rationalistic, narcissistic, mechanistic) were first presented as limitations of an inner imagination understanding. It was argued that these limitations fostered an abstracted distance from imaginative experience, one that poorly served the value that image-based therapists place upon experiential work. The subsequent presentation of an embodied, immersive, and animistic imagination that is ecological and fractal went on to address these limitations, sketching out a theory and practice aligned to the experiential ground of imagining in psychotherapy and everyday life.

The following four aspects of a transpersonal imagination as **non-dual**, **transrational**, **participatory**, and **emergent** present both a general summary of the points raised in the book and a specific image-centric alternative to each of the four limitations of inner imagining.

Non-Dual

Transpersonal imagining is a non-dual synthesis of the subjective and objective poles of experience—a non-duality that recognizes the indivisible nature of imagining and in which images are not mental objects, either contained within the mind or projected onto the world, but perceptions arising in between self and world. This is the non-dual territory that Carl Jung reclaimed as the meaning of "soul" and "psyche" (as discussed in chapter 3). It is also what psychoanalyst Donald Winnicott spoke of as a "third place",[26] where inner and outer realities overlap, and what Jungian analyst Nathan Schwartz-Salant described as an "interactive field"[27] of imaginal relations rather than individual projections.

A non-dual transpersonal imagining allows for a language and understanding that acknowledges the activity of images in everyday lived experience instead of a dualistic concern with the withdrawal of projections to a source within—an understanding that focuses upon the enhancement of self and world coming together, cultivating an embodied imaginal sensitivity to the shifting sensory impressions of people, places, and things, as was introduced in chapters 1 and 2.

Transrational

"Transrational" is a term popularized by the Jungian analyst Jerome Bernstein to describe "experience that does not readily fit into standard cause and effect logical structure".[28] A transpersonal imagining is transrational in that it does not reach after causal explanations and ideas, but instead, embraces the ambiguous, strange, and unexpected, without rushing prematurely into interpretations. The effect of this is a healing immersion within the experiential immediacy of imaginative process, rather than abstract ideas or retrospective thinking-about the content of what has been imagined.

That said, a transrational imagining is not without thought. The synthesis of transpersonal imagining includes all the psychological faculties, including thinking responses to the imagery. What is avoided is the eclipsing of imaginal perception by a narrow focus upon analytical thinking about what the imagery means, which removes us from the process of imagining. Instead, the experiential meaningfulness of transrational imagining is found in imagination itself as primary, rather than treating it as only a symbolic representation of ideas about meaning to be found elsewhere, as we saw in chapters 3 and 4.

Participatory

Transpersonal imagining is a participation within a process of imaginal activity. As we saw in chapter 3, to imagine is to find ourselves in a place. Instead of images being inside us, it is we who live surrounded by an imaginal environment—whether in the absorption of a movie or novel, in an "eyes-closed" waking dream, or walking down a city street. Without assuming images to be inner objects or psychological sub-parts, a transpersonal imagining, as we saw in chapters 5 and 6, allows for an animistic personification of all images as autonomous others, wild and free, not owned and controlled.

It is an interactive imaginal relationship, or what Jorge N. Ferrer calls a "participatory event",[29] one that recollects the *participation mystique* of Levy-Bruhl mentioned in chapter 5. It is a profoundly co-creative paradigm, one that decentralizes the habitual ego as an image amongst images, the effect of which is a healing, rather than exaccerbation, of our narcissism.

Emergent

Transpersonal imagining is emergent; there is no game plan or schedule to follow. Instead of a mechanistic or deterministic manufacturing of desired psychological change, seeking to control the *contents* of what is imagined, transpersonal imagining shifts our attention towards the *processes* active in healing and transformation. It is an imagining that focuses upon a synthesis of fine-grained attention to small and unexpected details, the developments of which are recognized as a creation, or "emergence", of something qualitatively new, as we saw in chapters 9 and 10.

A Lost Imagination

This chapter, as a conclusion to the whole book, has been about the "something missing" from my psychotherapy training, and also more broadly, a lost understanding of imagination.

The idea of a non-dual, transrational, participatory, and emergent transpersonal imagination is leaps and bounds away from the modern common-sense assumption, reflected in dictionary definitions, of imagination as a personal psychological interiority separated off from the surrounding world. At best this inner imagination is a partial understanding, one that has been shown to place serious limitations upon both therapeutic practice and the possibilities of imaginative life in general.

The modern view of imagination is a collective amnesia, a forgetting of a whole way of being and world view. To grow up in a culture that fails to take dreaming seriously, and dismisses imaginal encounters in everyday life as silly childhood make-believe, inevitably results in an adulthood loss of imaginative ability, a loss that has been shown to be a root cause of the rising tide of mental suffering in modern life. It is a loss that is all the more painful for being unacknowledged: firstly, in being presented as a developmental step forward to be celebrated rather than grieved; and secondly, in not having a name for that which we have lost, let alone a route map to find it again.

My hope is that this book has offered more than just a route map. The intention all along has been to offer a theoretical basis and practical method for the actual recovery of this lost imagination—as recollected in the proximate loss of childhood imagining and the ancestral loss of pre-modern imagining that secretly inspired the development of transpersonal psychotherapy.

In taking advantage of developments in contemporary science, the abrupt separation of subject and object, inner and outer, has been shown to be itself a fiction, an empiricism that we are no longer beholden to. This opportunity has allowed me to sketch out the principles of an image-centric approach to psychotherapy and everyday life, in which imagination is broadly conceived as the perception of images arising in between self and world.

In closing, it needs to be acknowledged that, both as writer and reader, we have come a long way in these pages. We have been on a journey together, re-imagining the possibilities of imagination. But now we come to the end, and I would like to take this opportunity to thank you for your time and attention, which has meant a lot to me. The at-times lonely effort of writing is ultimately made worthwhile when a book comes to life in the hands of a reader. It has been your imagination that has filled in the gaps left by the marks on the page and conjured a world of colourful pictures and stories, feelings and ideas. As we now part company and go our separate ways, all that remains is for me to wish you well in your onward travels. May you notice and follow novel images into an ever richer, story-filled, and enchanted life.

1. Jorge N. Ferrer. *Revisioning Transpersonal Theory: A Participatory Vision of Human Spirituality, Foreword by Richard Tarnas* (State University of New York Press, 2001), xv.

2. John Firman and Ann Gila, *Psychosynthesis: A Psychology of the Spirit* (State University of New York Press, 2002), 1.

3. Ibid, 1.

4. Ibid, 96.

5. Roberto Assagioli, *Transpersonal Inspiration and Psychological Mountain Climbing, Reprint No. 38* (New York: Psychosynthesis Research Foundation, 1976).

6. Roberto Assagioli, *The Act of Will* (New York: Penguin Books, 1973), 46.

7. Roberto Assagioli,*Psychosynthesis: A Manual of Principles and Techniques* (London: Thorsons, 1993), 21, 26, 29, 204, 206.

8. John Firman & Ann Gila, *Psychosynthesis: A Psychology of the Spirit* (State University of New York Press, 2002), 129, 132, 140.

9. Piero Ferrucci, *What We May Be: Techniques for Psychological and Spiritual Growth through Psychosynthesis* (New York: Tarcher Putnam, 1982), 144.

10. Allan Frater, "The Imagination Imagined" (unpublished Master of Arts Dissertation in Psychosynthesis Psychotherapy, validated by University of East London, UK, 2011).

11. Jean Hardy, *A Psychology with Soul: Psychosynthesis in Evolutionary Context* (Woodgrange Press: London, UK, 1996), 97.

12. Jorge N. Ferrer, *Revisioning Transpersonal Theory: A Participatory Vision of Human Spirituality* (State University of New York Press, 2001), 30.

13. Ibid, 9.

14. Ibid, 20.

15. Roberto Assagioli, "Talks on the Self: a Conversation" handout (London: The Psychosynthesis and Education Trust), n.d.

16. Jean Hardy, *A Psychology with Soul: Psychosynthesis in Evolutionary Context* (Woodgrange Press: London, UK, 1996), 2.

17. https://psychosynthesistrust.org.uk/beyond-wall-silence-psychosynthesis-inside/

18. Jorge N. Ferrer, *Revisioning Transpersonal Theory: A Participatory Vision of Human Spirituality* (State University of New York Press, 2001), 116.

19. John Firman, *'I' and Self: Re-visioning Psychosynthesis* (Psychosynthesis Palo Alto, California, USA, 2020), 19.

20. Roberto Assagioli, *Psychosynthesis: A Manual of Principles and Techniques* (London: Thorsons, 1993), 122.

21. Jorge N. Ferrer, *Revisioning Transpersonal Theory: A Participatory Vision of Human Spirituality* (State University of New York Press, 2001), 125.

22. Roberto Assagioli, Psychosynthesis: *A Manual of Principles and Techniques* (London: Thorsons, 1993), 22.

23. Robert Bosnak, *Embodiment: Creative Imagination in Medicine, Art and Travel* (Abbingdon, Oxon.: Routledge, 2007), 22 (quote).

24. Richard Tarnas, *Cosmos and Psyche: Intimations of a New World View* (Plume, Published by Penguin Group, New York, USA, 2007), 16-25.

25. Diana Whitmore, *Psychosynthesis Counselling in Action* (London: Sage Publications, 2000), 18.

26. Madeleine Davis and David Wallbridge, *Boundaries and Space: An Introduction to the work of D. W. Winnicott* (Karnac Books Ltd, London, UK, 1981), 160.

27. Nathan Schwartz-Salant, *The Borderline Personality* (Chiron Publications, Asheville, NC, USA, 1989), 110.

28. Jerome Bernstein, *Living in the Borderland: The Evolution of Consciousness and the Challenge of Healing Trauma* (Routledge, East Sussex, UK, 2005), xv, xvi.

29. Jorge N. Ferrer, *Revisioning Transpersonal Theory: A Participatory Vision of Human Spirituality* (State University of New York Press, 2001), 115.

Bibliography

Abram, David. *Becoming Animal: An Earthly Cosmology* (New York: Penguin Random House, 2011).

Abram, David. *The Spell of the Sensuous* (New York: Vintage Books, 1997).

Assagioli, Roberto. *Psychosynthesis: A Manual of Principles and Techniques* (London: Thorsons, 1993).

Assagioli, Roberto. *Transpersonal Inspiration and Psychological Mountain Climbing, Reprint No. 38* (New York: Psychosynthesis Research Foundation, 1976).

Assagioli, Roberto. *The Act of Will* (New York: Penguin Books, 1973).

Berger, John. *Ways of Seeing* (London: Penguin Press, 2008).

Bernstein, Jerome. *Living in the Borderland: The Evolution of Consciousness and the Challenge of Healing Trauma* (Routledge, East Sussex, UK, 2005).

Bettelheim, Bruno. *The Uses of Enchantment: The Meaning and Importance of Fairy Tales* (New York: Penguin Press, 1991).

Blaffer Hardy, Sarah. *Mothers and Others: The Evolutionary Origins of Mutual Understanding* (Cambridge, MA: Harvard University Press, 2009).

Bookchin, Murray. *The Ecology of Freedom: The Emergence and Dissolution of Hierarchy* (Chico, CA: AK Press, 2005).

Bosnak, Robert. *A Little Course In Dreams* (Berkeley, CA: Shambhala, 1986).

Bosnak, Robert. *Embodiment: Creative Imagination in Medicine, Art and Travel* (Abbingdon, Oxon.: Routledge, 2007).

Bosnak, Robert. *Tracks in the Wilderness of Dreaming: Exploring Interior Landscape Through Practical Dreamwork* (New York: Dell Publishing, 1996)

Boulton, Jean G. *Embracing Complexity: Strategic Perspectives for an Age of Turbulence* (Oxford University Press, 2015).

Brody, Hugh. *The Other Side of Eden: Hunters, Farmers, and the Shaping of the World* (New York: North Point Press, 2000).

Brody, Hugh. *Maps and Dreams* (London: Faber and Faber, 2002).

Buhner, Stephen Harrod. *Plant Intelligence and the Imaginal Realm* (Rochester, VT: Bear & Company/Inner Traditions, 2014).

Cregan-Reid, Vybarr. *Footnotes*: *How Running Makes Us Human* (London: Ebury Publishing, 2017).

Dargert, Guy. *The Snake in the Clinic: Psychotherapy's Role in Medicine and Healing* (London: Karnac, 2016).

Davis, Madeleine and David Wallbridge, *Boundaries and Space: An Introduction to the work of D. W. Winnicott* (Karnac Books Ltd, London, UK, 1981).

Doerr, Anthony. *Four Seasons in Rome: On Twins, Insomnia and the Biggest Funeral in the History of the World* (New York: Scribner, 2008).

Feder, Jens. *Fractals* (Switzerland: Springer Science and Business Media, 2013).

Fee, Angie. *Sexuality and Gender* seminar (London: The Psychosynthesis Trust, circa 2004).

Ferrer, Jorge N. *Revisioning Transpersonal Theory: A Participatory Vision of Human Spirituality* (State University of New York Press, 2001).

Ferrucci, Piero. *What We May Be: Techniques for Psychological and Spiritual Growth through Psychosynthesis* (New York: Tarcher Putnam, 1982).

Fesmire, Steven. *Ecological Imagination in Moral Education*, East and West. (Annales Philosophici, 2011).

Firman, John. *'I' and Self: Re-visioning Psychosynthesis* (Psychosynthesis Palo Alto, California, USA, 2020).

Firman, John and Ann Gila, *Psychosynthesis: A Psychology of the Spirit* (State University of New York Press, 2002).

Fisher, Andy. *Radical Ecopsychology: Psychology in the Service of Life* (Albany: State University of New York Press, 2013).

Galatzer-Levy, Robert M. *Nonlinear Psychoanalysis: Notes from Forty Years of Chaos and Complexity Theory* (Abbingdon, Oxon.: Routledge, 2017).

Gold, Joseph. *The Story Species: Our Life-Literature Connection* (Markham, Ontario, Canada: Fitzhenry and Whiteside, 2002).

Graeber, David. *Direct Action: An Ethnography* (Edinburgh: AK Press, 2009).

Graeber, David. *Possibilities: Essays on Hierarchy, Rebellion, and Desire* (Edinburgh: AK Press, 2007).

Graeber, David. *Fragments of an Anarchist Anthropology* (Chicago: Prickly Paradigm Press, 2004).

Griffiths, Jay. *Kith: The Riddle of the Childscape* (London: Penguin Press, 2013).

Hardy, Jean. *A Psychology with Soul: Psychosynthesis in Evolutionary Context* (Woodgrange Press: London, UK, 1996).

Harvey, Graham. *Animism: Respecting the Living World, 2nd ed.* (London: Hurst, 2017).

Hillman, James. "Image-Sense", in *Working with Images: The Theoretical Base of Archetypal Psychology*, ed. Benjamin Sells (Thompson, CT: Spring Publications, 2000),

Hillman, James. *Re-Visioning Psychology* (New York: Harper Perennial, 1992).

Hillman, James. *The Myth of Analysis* (New York: Harper Perennial, 1972).

Hillman, James. *We've had a hundred years of psychotherapy and the world's getting worse* (New York: Harper Perennial, 1992).

Hopkins, Rob. *From What Is to What If: Unleashing the Power of Imagination to Create the Future We Want* (London: Chelsea Green Publishing, 2019).

Jung, Carl. *The Archetypes and the Collective Unconscious* (Collected Works, Vol. 9, Part I).

Kane, Sean. *Wisdom of the Mythtellers* (Ontario: Broadview Press, 1998).

Lachman, Gary. *Lost Knowledge of the Imagination* (Edinburgh, Scotland: Floris Books, 2017).

Lakoff, George and Mark Johnson. *Metaphors We Live By* (University of Chicago Press, 2003).

Levine, Stephen K. *Trauma, Tragedy, Therapy: The Arts and Human Suffering* (London: Jessica Kingsley, 2009).

Lockhart, Russell. *Psyche Speaks: A Jungian Approach to Self and World* (Everett, WA: The Lockhart Press, 2014).

Lockhart, Russell and Paco Mitchell. *Dreams, Bones & the Future: A Dialogue* (Owl and Heron Press, 2015).

Manjusvara. *Writing Your Way* (Cambridge, UK: Windhorse Publications, 2005).

Marks-Tarlow, Terry. *Psyche's Veil: Psychotherapy, Fractals and Complexity* (Abbingdon, Oxon.: Routledge, 2008).

Modell, Arnold H. *Imagination and the Meaningful Brain* (Cambridge, MA: MIT Press, 2003).

Murdoch, Iris. *Existentialists and Mystics* (London: Penguin Press, 1999).

Murphy, Peter, Michael A. Peters, et al. *Imagination: Three Models of Imagination in the Age of the Knowledge Economy* (Bern, Switzerland: Peter Lang Publishing, 2010).

Nelson, Richard K. *Make Prayers to the Raven: A Koyukon View of the Northern Forest* (University of Chicago Press, 1983).

Philips, James and James Morley, ed. *Imagination and its Pathologies* (Cambridge, MA: The MIT Press, 2003).

Powers, Richard. *The Overstory* (New York: Norton, 2019).

Pullman, Philip. *The Secret Commonwealth: The Book of Dust, Volume Two* (London: Penguin, 2020).

Restall Orr, Emma. *The Wakeful World: Animism, Mind and the Self in Nature* (New Alresford, UK: Moon Books/John Hunt Publishing, 2012).

Robertson, Chris. *Transformation in Troubled Times: Re-Vision's Soulful Approach to Therapeutic Work* (Forres, Scotland: TransPersonal Press, 2018).

Rollo, May. *Love and Will* (New York: W.W.Norton & Company, 2007).

Romanyshyn, Robert. *Psychological Life: From Science to Metaphor* (Milton Keynes: The Open University Press, 1982).

Roszak, Theodore. *The Voice of the Earth: An Exploration of Ecopsychology* (Grand Rapids, MI: Phanes Press, 2001).

Roszak, Theodore , Mary E. Gomes, and Allen D. Kanner, Ed. *Ecopsychology: Restoring the Earth, Healing the Mind*, Ed. (Berkeley, CA: Counterpoint Press, 1995).

Rowan, John. *Subpersonalities: The People inside Us* (Abbingdon, Oxon.: Routledge, 1990).

Rowson, Jonathan. *The Moves that Matter: A Chess Grandmaster on the Game of Life* (London: Bloomsbury Publishing, 2019).

Sahlins, Marshall, *Stone Age Economics* (Abbingdon, Oxon.: Routledge, 2017).

Schwartz-Salant, Nathan. *The Borderline Personality: Vision and Healing* (Asheville, NC: Chiron Publications, 1989).

Scott, James C. *Against the Grain: A Deep History of the Earliest States* (New Haven, CT: Yale University Press, 2017).

Sells, Benjamin, ed. *Working with Images: The Theoretical Base of Archetypal Psychology* (Thompson, CT: Spring Publications, 2000).

Shamadasani, S. *Jung and the Making of Modern Psychology: The Dream of a Science* (Cambridge University Press, 2003).

Stein, Zachary. *Education in a Time between Worlds: Essays on the Future of Schools, Technology, and Society* (San Francisco, CA: Bright Alliance, 2019).

Stern, Daniel N. *The Present Moment in Psychotherapy and Everyday Life* (New York: W.W. Norton & Company, 2014).

Stewart, I. *Does God Play Dice?* (New York: Blackwell, 2002).

Tarnas, Richard. *Cosmos and Psyche: Intimations of a New World View* (New York: Plume/Penguin Group, 2007).

Taylor, Mark C. *The Moment of Complexity: Emerging Network Culture* (University of Chicago Press, 2001).

Totton, Nick. *Wild Therapy: Undomesticating Outer and Inner Worlds* (Ross-on-Wye: PCCS Book, 2011).

Watkins, Mary. *Invisible Guests* (Thompson, CT: Spring Publications, 2000).

Watkins, Mary. *Waking Dreams* (Thompson, CT: Spring Publications, 2003).

Wheatley, Margaret. *Leadership and the New Science: Discovering Order in a Chaotic World* (Oakland, CA: Berrett-Koehler Publishers, 2006).

Whitmore, Diana. *Psychosynthesis Counselling in Action* (London: Sage Publications, 2000).

Acknowledgements

There are many to whom I owe a debt of gratitude for their inspiration and support during the writing of this book. In particular, the staff and students, past and present, of the Psychosynthesis Trust, who provided me with a context to discuss and clarify my ideas, without which this book would probably never have come about. I would also like to thank my wife, Bethany, who has provided a reliable place of shelter, welcome rest, and companionship on what has been at times a difficult and lonely journey. A thousand thanks also go to my team of intrepid readers (Tim, Sophia, Jasper, Ryan and Robert) for their belief in the book in its early stages and the generous wisdom and wit they shared to help bring it to fruition. Keith Robinson also needs a special mention for his wonderful cover illustration that captures so well the spirit of the book. The team at Transpersonal Press also need a special mention: Stacey, for championing the development of transpersonal psychotherapy and giving me the opportunity to write the book; Thierry, for his calm, straightforward guidance and patience; and Nicky, for her astute and fine-grained edits. And last but not least, thank you, dear reader, for bringing the book to life with your time and attention, which means a lot to me.

About the Author

Allan Frater grew up on the edge of a small village near Edinburgh, reading comics and walking his dog Jet in the surrounding countryside. He survived an engineering degree and a failed career as a maths teacher by watching movies and reading novels. Inspired by Jack Kerouac and Herman Hesse, he spent his twenties living and working in Buddhist communities where he came across the east-meets-west fusion of transpersonal psychology and eventually trained to become a psychotherapist. His psychotherapy practice and teaching career at the Psychosynthesis Trust have researched the meeting place between transpersonal psychology and an image-based approach to ecotherapy, the results of which are presented in this book. Now living in North London, married and middle-aged, he feels fortunate to have kept touch with his original sources of inspiration, continuing to read comics and spend time outdoors walking his dog Milly.

Index

Also available

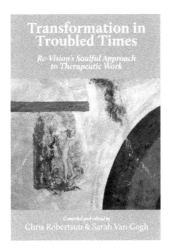

To celebrate its 30 years of pioneering work in the fields of counselling and psychotherapy training, the Re-Vision Centre for Transpersonal & Integrative Therapy has brought together a selection of writing by practitioners and teachers who have worked at the heart of the organization.

The chapters address a social and cultural crisis which, at this point in the history of our planet, needs new ways of looking at therapy and how it relates to the world beyond the consulting room. Just as 'the personal is political' was a way of seeing individual issues within the context of a wider political field, so we now need to see that the soul is a different kind of agency from that of the ego – one that is both internal and external, individual and cultural. The world may have lost connection with soul in its obsession with merchandise and control, but soul has not lost connection with us. These chapters offer an integrative perspective that both gives a place to the troubles of the modern world and also develops a well-tuned craft to firstly attend to our painful wounds and ultimately transform their bitterness into the salt of wisdom.

This book is a compelling work for psychotherapists, counsellors, trainees, and anyone interested in how psychotherapy influences and is influenced by the state of the planet, by imagination and by the reality of how politics impact on our daily lives.

ISBN 978-1-912-618-02-8 (print) / 978-1-912618-03-5 (ebook)

TransPersonal
Press

Also available

Transpersonal Dynamics offers approaches to the therapeutic encounter from the leading edge of quantum physics field theory and integrative psychology.

Transpersonal Dynamics is the culmination of over 20 years of feedback about 'what works', gathered through delivering integrative and transpersonal training to counsellors, coaches, psychologists and psychotherapists who work with organisations, adults, couples, families, young people and children.

Using down-to-earth language in a practical way, this book addresses some of the gritty aspects of the therapeutic relationship, with the aim to inspire and support practitioners to take more risks to bring a collaborative, relational quality to their work.

Stacey Millichamp is a trainer on the Masters Degree in Psychotherapy and the Diploma in Integrative and Transpersonal Clinical Supervision at the Psychosynthesis Trust *in London, and teaches on the Diploma in Supervision with Soul at the* Re-Vision Centre for Integrative Psychosynthesis *in London. She is the Director of* Entrust Associates, *which provides counselling to staff and students of secondary and primary schools in London.*

isbn 978-1-912-618-00-4 (print) / 978-1-912618-00-1 (ebook)

TransPersonal
Press

Also available

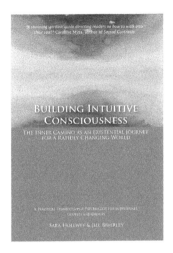

Are you looking to make real and lasting change in your life? *Building Intuitive Consciousness* offers a reliable and effective method to support such change by guiding readers on an inner pilgrimage to awaken to their Intuitive Consciousness.

It has been said that no problem can be solved from the same level of consciousness that created it. We believe that by awakening to the Intuitive Consciousness within ourselves, we are able to transcend old patterns and habitual behaviours that may be limiting us in some way from being able to take our next steps forward.

Using the wisdom of ancient spiritual practice and modern psychology, *Building Intuitive Consciousness* is both a practical and mystical manual to guide you on this journey. By delving deep into our psychology and expanding up into the heights of our numinous or spiritual potential, this unsentimental book offers a roadmap to access our true inner wisdom, free from the restraints and distortions of our ego.

Packed with immediately applicable insights and accessible exercises, this second edition now includes notes that are relevant for professionals, making it the perfect manual for psychologists, therapists, managers or anyone on a journey of self-discovery.

isbn 978-1-912-618-04-2 (print) / 978-1-912618-05-9 (ebook)

TransPersonal
Press

Also available

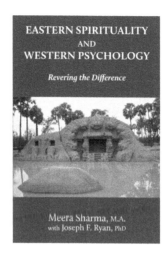

Eastern Spirituality and Western Psychology offers a practical path to harmony between spirituality and Western psychology, between heart and mind.
  This book:
  • challenges basic assumptions of Western psychology
  • demystifies Vedic psychology
  • presents how Eastern spirituality can enhance Western psychology
  It guides readers by clarifying the relationship between spirituality and psychological growth, and demonstrates that psychotherapy and spirituality are complementary aspects of human development, with both essential for optimum mental, existential, and spiritual growth. It is up to everyone to take responsibility for making the changes that enable us to contribute to the well-being of the whole.
  In this insightful book, the authors reflect on this revolution and consider how it is likely to evolve in the future. It paves the way for those interested in the transpersonal, whether psychologists, psychotherapists, Orientalists, or spiritual practitioners.

isbn 978-1-912-618-06-6 (print) / 978-1-912618-07-3 (ebook)

TransPersonal
Press